"I LOVE TO HATE FASHION"

"I LOVE TO HATE FASHION"

Real Quotes and Whispers Behind the Runway

LOÏC PRIGENT

CERNUNNOS

Translation (from French): Gabriel Quincey

Many thanks to Damian Thompson for his invaluable advice and suggestions.

ISBN: 978-2-37495-085-3

Printed and bound in the U.S.A.
10 9 8 7 6 5 4 3 2 1

Texts: Loïc Prigent
Cernunnos logo design: Mark Ryden
Book design: Shawn Dahl, dahlimama inc

Abrams books are available at special discounts when purchased in quantity
for premiums and promotions as well as fundraising or educational use.

Special editions can also be created to specification. For details, contact
specialsales@abramsbooks.com or the address below.

ABRAMS The Art of Books
195 Broadway, New York, NY 10007
abramsbooks.com

CONTENTS

INTRODUCTION

"It was so awesome that I remember nothing."

I won't give any names. OK, fine, it's Karl, it's Donatella, it's Anna, it's me, it's the intern, it's the assistant at full blast. It's the extremely out-of-sync Italian couturier, it's my comrade Leo in top form on a terrace; it's PR, the hairdresser, the designer, the fanatic personal assistant, the couture oil-moneyed customer. It's the editor who thinks she is discreet when she has 15,000 dollars' worth of clothes on her back (for she has paid nothing, she is not aware of cost). "Everything has been said, and we have come too late, now that man has been thinking for seven thousand years and more," said La Bruyere . . . Thinking, dressing, and living in Paris.

"She is beautiful, but we need to do something about the forehead." When this sentence was spoken in front of me in a studio, no one reacted. The model, not even twenty years old, remained frozen, unmoved by this verdict. The great couturier who had said it didn't think twice about discussing her in the third person. All the great professionals present approved, and the makeup artist took a brush and some matte foundation and went about erasing the forehead. The girl took three steps and, finally, she had become beautiful. No one laughed or found this cruel; it was just the process of seeking perfection.

My job is to listen to these people talk. And note their words for posterity. I like to film with a handheld camera, discreetly, more or less forgotten. I like to laugh with them, take advantage of their fanciful thought system. During fashion shows, I laugh from morning to night. "I am on a diet of bottled water and stolen candy from Ubers." I love the shows where everyone is happy to be in a bad mood. I might even like the excessive vibes. We are in a bubble of a bubble; we moan about getting hit on by Pharrell Williams. The problem with privilege is that we quickly become addicts—when you taste luxury, you always want more. These sentences become a meditation on excess, but above all, a good laugh (like we say at Chanel).

I was in a cutting room with Julie, an editor colleague, and we laughed out loud at the playful madness of what a famous designer had said on film the day before, behind the scenes of his show. But now, with the report finished, the words had been dulled, ready to be swallowed and consumed, hardly noticed, reduced to bizarre babbling whose meaning has been lost in the edit. Frustrated, we resolved to find a way to underline the funniest statements, without malice, to elevate them to the level of proverbs, amazing and raw, about fashion. We wrote the quotes in a huge font on the screen, effectively capturing the designer's glibness in full measure. Transcribing the words of fashion people has become a habit after that.

"I love fashion, but it's also everything I hate." The context in which this sentence was pronounced is absurd—an unlikely person, no doubt as cultured as he is insane. I could tell the whole anecdote—frankly, it is funny—but I tell myself that it is more interesting to leave this sentence out of context. It was said seriously, not in jest, as were most of the quotes in this book. Of course, I understood what this person wanted to say: Fashion is too hostile to be loved in full, and even if we do want to be part of this select club, we know that it will require sacrifices, including preconceptions of propriety, decency, and possibly bank accounts. "Am I bothering you?" "No, it's OK, I was thinking of Prada."

The joy of fashion is its soulless appearance. We groom ourselves to ecstasy; we reject reality as a useless ballast. In this world, "normal" does not exist. The more artificial the better. Renew anything older than five minutes. "She has done a lot of things to her skin. Now her face is behind her skull." Everything is overstated, more or less unconsciously. Noting these words is also sharing a secret; a sophisticated form of recklessness. Proof that there are still fanatics living the dream of Madame de Pompadour.

It's a good party whether we hear three wonderful gems rejecting common sense or a thousand. We take note, laugh, and forget them all the day after.

Like the émigrés of Koblenz, these gossipmongers have learned everything and forgotten nothing. Their days are dizziness. Are they right? Are they wrong? They are the frivolous and serious birds of a unique jungle: "Welcome to the best-dressed mental asylum of the world."

—Loïc Prigent

SEASON 2013

"It's not that I'm late, it's that I live
on Greenwich Mean Time and a half."

"Yes, she does wear a lot of perfume.
We named her 'Sephora Has Exploded.'"

"He's not into mental dexterity
but he is crazy charming."

"I want comfort after all.
I'm sick of putting up with my clothes."

"The collection was funny!"
"Yes, but we don't want to be funny.
We want to be beautiful."

"You know, the world is divided
into two groups:
rubes and big rubes."

"I couldn't get involved with a guy
who wears V-neck T-shirts."

"I just saw Thierry Mugler in person."

"I wanted yesterday to last a lifetime."

"Your fantasy just called, it says it's OK."

"Enjoy your weekend,
but most of all, enjoy you."

"You should never pose near a column.
You don't want to be thinner
nor thicker than the column."

"Do you have a synonym for *stripe*?
It's only the first day,
and I'm totally repeating myself already."

"Yes, I eat. I take vitamin C in the morning."
(said with the utmost sincerity)

"Hey, Nicolas Ghesquière sent me a text."

"I love watching
how real people dress."

"The trick is to know whether the H&M fashion show
is going to copy Celine or Saint Laurent.
Can you imagine the H&M fashion show not copying you?
Embarrassing."

"Being fat is awesome, your face
is puffy and you don't have wrinkles anymore."

"His shows were pretty awesome,
until he started to think.
Now I don't go anymore."

"She tweets so much;
it's like her fingers have got diarrhea."

"My roommate's a chef, but he got fired by Valentino
because he messed up Anne Hathaway's soufflé."

"I was as drunk
as an English model."

"It's always sad when the audience isn't applauding
and you can hear the backstage crew
screaming with joy."

"We were in a strategic meeting when Miuccia Prada
started yelling at her husband."

"We are exhausted.
Anything we say becomes untweetable."

"Do you think these harem pants catch fire easily?"

"He also Celined the point well."

"In the past the whole room would rush
to kiss him at the end of the fashion show.
Now he's getting two kisses
with three Russian nouveau riches."

"Her dad has Warhol's paintings
like your dad has socks."

"My driver is so endearing."

"For my fortieth birthday
let's have a party in a barge and sink it."

"This house is getting somewhere
thanks to caffeine
and the ambitions of the interns."

"I went vegetarian.
If I have to, I could order
a steak tartare, but that's it."

"Yesterday I was having dinner with rich people
who were talking about Paris.
It took me forever to realize
they were talking about the city in Texas."

"He's ugly. He's got an ugly nose.
He turns me on."

"They're all going to be wearing black Valentino again.
It's the return of the clone-bitches."

"Last season I was embroidering
with sunglasses on because it was just so terrible."

"The schedule is insane.
Monday, I have ten dinners."

"You don't think the collection is sexy enough?
Apart from making a hole in the back of the skirts
I don't see how we can get sexier."

"One gets used to luxury.
It's awful."

"I just bought Colette Adidas sneakers by Raf Simons.
They are so horrible.
I love them."

"She listens to client A's ideas and client B's ideas.
Then she makes them doubt their ideas,
but then she saves them by selling B's idea to A
and vice versa. Genius."

"I know you don't eat
but at least take a mint."

"Oh, you've shed, that's wonderful!"

"The moon is low and huge."
"Just like your ass."

"If you look rested when you get back from your vacation,
it was a failure."

"You don't say *she takes too much speed*;
you say *she is translucent*."

"You don't say *heavy*,
you say *unexpected silhouette*."

"You don't say *depressive*, you say *client*."

"I'm utterly wrecked."

"Let me in."
"But who are you?"
"Google me."

"You're mean. I forgot
that you got mean twice a year
during the fashion shows.
See you in eight days."

"My boss used to give us her second-row seats,
but now that she's getting third row,
I think she's burning her invitations."

"Since her collections became ugly,
her profits have multiplied ten times over."

"The inspiration is a real woman,
but a Balmain reality."

"How old is she?"
"Impossible to say. She gets these tricky facelifts
where the surgeon leaves only fake wrinkles."

"In my phone
I saved her as Satan."

"I had an optic burnout."

"I'm too lazy to go to
Pharrell Williams's party at Castel."

"Are you OK, love?"
(to a terrified intern)

"We had a budget of $300,000
for the last fashion show's embroidery,
but it was a hit, so they took off the limit."

"The inspiration is a woman who works.
And who has five vacation homes."

"Jason Statham was at Balmain.
He's five feet tall."

"He wanted to get fired, so he came
to the studio in a salmon-pink suit for a month."

"He's got a salary of a million a month."
"Gross or net?"

"They dressed the girls too early, and as a result
they walked on the runway with sweaty armpits."

"Want a banana? It's fatty but it's good."

"Ah, I see we've all received
the same gorgeous bag . . ."

"The inspiration is a woman
who dresses in a formal way
to go to the beach."

"My son just brought a sewing machine home."
"Oh shit . . ."

"I cry every night until 6 AM,
but during the day, I feel great."

"The collection is hideous.
We can't even photograph it.
We'll be forced to make a
full-page spread with the bag again."

"His assistant sent a resignation email
with three words: 'Better elsewhere. Ciao.'"
"Assistants have gotten worse than us."

"He wanted to try BDSM,
except he created his leather outfit
with his head seamstress,
who made it with gorgeous dipped lambskin."

"I have a pimple as big as the Dior poster
on Place Vendôme."

"I love her!"
"But isn't she a bit mean?"
"Yes, a bit."
"A bit?"
"Yes, OK, she is a bitch.
But I love her."

"He invented the $500 T-shirt.
He's a genius."

"We tried to re-create the full effect of the vintage clothing
we were inspired by. Impossible.
So, we put the vintage clothing on the runway instead."

"I just realized
all of my best friends are
press agents."

"Oh, are you wearing the Saint Laurent
tartan shirt? It's the first time
I've seen it in real life."

"Is she a press agent or a journalist?"
"I don't know. They're kind of the same, aren't they?"

"He's the nicest, most elegant guy
in Paris, but his breath stinks. An absolute stench.
He's Pepé le Pew Brummell."

"The collection was so bitchy.
I say *bitch*, but it's not pejorative when I say it."

"Walk faster, girls!
Walk like you're going too fast!"

"He's the Austrian Helmut Lang!"
"Uh, Helmut Lang is Austrian . . ."

"No! Take off your makeup and do the eye again.
It has to look badly done."

"I'm taking Kanye West to the bathroom
and coming back."
(shouted over a walkie-talkie)

"Basically, our client today
is a twenty-three-year-old woman from Kazakhstan
whose husband wears leather jackets."

"The inspiration is a nineties girl
with platform shoes
who wants to be unhappy."

"The hype around him died out so quickly.
I hope he hasn't ditched his real friends
in the meantime."

"The inspiration is a Parisian girl
who goes to Arizona and then comes back to Paris
to destroy her mother's wardrobe."

"There I am, in the marathon phase
where I don't even miss real life anymore."

"The inspiration is the fight
against overfishing the fishes
in the oceans."

"Listen, it's a thousand degrees and it reeks of plastic,
I'm calling you back after the fashion show."

"The trend is a morning gala outfit.
Morning is the new night."

"Have you heard? There's a modeling agency
called Monster."
"You call your mother to say, 'Mom,
I got signed to Monster.' That's real pride."

"The inspiration is a slut from Martha's Vineyard."

"They go broke for their accessories.
They carry their $2,000 bags
with nothing inside."

"I would like a plate of spinach."
"Sorry, the kitchen is closed."
"So what?"

"There's a TV channel asking me for the inspiration.
What do I say? Quick!"
(to the assistant, who immediately comes up
with a line that gets said on camera)

"The inspiration is Cher in Las Vegas,
but at a funeral."

"Were they real clothes at least?"
"Yes. Well, let's say for a real princess . . ."

"I know your job is to stop me
from getting in, but mine
is to get in anyway."

"Did you see? The marble is plastic."

"Vuitton? Bernard and Anna were standing.
Grace was crying. Lorenzo had a nervous breakdown."

"We laughed all night at the restaurant,
but at the end of the night, I realized he wasn't making
jokes but admitting really sad stuff to me."

"I feel like we are dead, and that they keep beating us up
with turquoise crocodile boots."

"Yesterday I was so tired, I made myself some pasta
but I forgot to put the pasta in the water."
"Good diet idea . . ."

"I couldn't sell luxury watches, having to stare
at the horrible skin of rich people's wrists all day long."

"My motto is put your money on your
wardrobe, put nothing in the bank."

"What about you, when was the first time you met Karl?"

"The new redneck is the $6,000 bag."

"Do you have sugar?"
"There is no sugar in this house."

"I can't believe I'm giving back all my
borrowed clothes tonight
and ending up with my own shit."

"I have a date but nothing is going to happen,
he's taken."
"We're in Paris, nobody's taken."

"Capitalism is addiction."

"In fact, old people go to Marrakech
the way we go to Berlin."

"She's crying, but it's normal.
We work in fashion, girls cry . . ."

"In her editorial, Anna Wintour said
that at the Met dinner
Jennifer Lawrence ate the food
Marion Cotillard left on her plate."

"I yelled at him for a good ten minutes.
That relaxed me."

"We were late to the movie *Blue Is the Warmest Color*.
We were in the front row, and the screen was giant.
We weren't hungry anymore when we got out."

"Jil Sander is a woman?
I thought she was a man.
Gilles Sander . . ."

"She has a Clarins face,
but a McDonald's body."

"We can't let that kind of product come out!
It's cheesy, ugly, and bad for the environment."
"You just described the brand's DNA."

"The risk with this kind of mink
is getting kidnapped because you look so rich.
But your family doesn't pay the ransom
because you're so ugly."

"It says 'looking for saleswomen,'
but if you ask me, they should also be looking for lawyers
given the number of fakes they sell."

"I'm depressed. It's December 1
and there are still no Christmas presents
for the editorial department. Not a chinchilla pillow, nothing."

"It used to be that starting in mid-November
the reception area would get clogged up
with Christmas presents."

"Nowadays, if you haven't given them the cover a dozen times,
the brands don't send anything
but an unsold scarf."

"My intern is lame. She does nothing all day.
She wouldn't even steal a Lanvin T-shirt.
I used to steal everything when I first got hired."

"New Year's Eve is only memorable
if you don't remember it the next morning."

SEASON 2014

"She's stingy. She'll be buried
in borrowed clothes."
"The press office will call the cemetery
to pick up the outfit."

"January 1, that brief moment in the year
when caramel and barbecue-flavored Pringles
are the antichrist."

"She is awful at interviewing people.
Asking questions this lousy is like
Shazam'ing old Madonna songs."

"She complains about life with
an iPhone in one hand and Starbucks in the other."

"The light in the Fendi store is golden,
and changes depending on the weather.
Best place to take selfies in Paris."

"And when you go out in Paris where do you go?"
"Berlin."

"The day before the shoot, the boss sent an email:
'The tiger is not fashionable enough.'
We had to recast a tiger overnight."

"I was forced to sign a nondisclosure agreement
promising that I would not describe this shoe to anyone."

"No, he doesn't give interviews.
The clothes speak for him."

"He doesn't have at all the Baudelaire way to take drugs;
he has the hairdressing one . . ."

"I put on a horrified expression when I'm texting,
so I don't look like I'm trying to ignore people.
That way, people hate me less on the subway."

"I put the 'out of office' auto-response
on my emails this morning. It's OK, it's Friday.
Six hours won't make a difference."

"We all know he's crazy, and he terrifies us.
We're waiting for someone from the outside
to film him in a Hitler moment and save us . . ."

"He's a Word Editor but at *Vogue USA*."

"The collection is super porn-y. The press service
had to spray crabs repellant
on the clothes before the shoots . . ."

"What do you do?"
"Data crunching."
"And what do you data crunch?"
"Data."

"He looks at me
the way my father looks at BMWs."

"She picked up her cell phone
during a fitting session with Karl."
"???"
"And she spoke."
"What????"

"Did you get that email from the Yves Klein Foundation
saying that we don't have the right to say *Klein blue* anymore?
They suggest *overseas blue* instead."

"She is a good consultant:
She removes the dresses that are too beautiful and would make
the other dresses look a bit bland."

"I entered as a tape assistant.
I would tape stuff.
Now with computers you don't tape
anymore, and I wouldn't have made a career."

"She's experiencing major depression, but she's a lot of fun."

"I'm off to a good start this year, except for my nails.
My nails are a disaster."

"My dress went to the fitting.
They said the fall of my fabric was 'too slow.'
Right now I'm going to cry in the bathroom,
and then do it all over again."

"He looked at me so super fiercely.
I think I'm pregnant from that look."

"It's an exceptional kind of poppers
that I developed myself in Grasse, France."

"Wait, does he really make poppers in Grasse?"

"So this fabric is made of black dots
but on a black background."
"So it's black."
"Yes, I guess you can say that."

"The next time she says 'my gift is intuition,'
I'm hitting her with the Guy Bourdin book
that she's been ripping off for thirty years."

"We shot a series of girls in golden swimwear
against a wall of tanned men.
They made for a wonderful texture
to the background."

"Your tomato is huge!"
"Yes, it's a Mugler tomato."

"You will be a proscenium guide."
"You mean I'm going to show
the models that they have to turn around
at the end of the catwalk?"

"His name is Pari but without an *S*."

"It's not vulgarity, it's impactful."

"No, an interview will not be possible,
but do you want to film the installation
of the cushions on Tuesday at 8 AM?"

"I took a selfie with Donatella,
but I wouldn't dare post it."

"It was so outdated that the prices
on the labels were in francs."

"She is incredibly toxic. She would make a great muse."

"He's an economist."
(speaking of a CEO)

"I ate too much!"
"Stop, you ate half an apple . . ."

"Frankly, I wouldn't have been friends
with my daughter in school.
She doesn't dress well enough . . ."

"Sugar! Our red carpet is empty.
We've got a muse emergency."

"Beware.
The nicer they are, the meaner they are."

"Your driver is lovely. Mine speaks."

"Yeah, he's OK.
But when he finally breaks free from his shitty good taste,
he will be brilliant."

"It was horribly pretentious."
"You don't usually mind that, though."

"He's handsome.
He's a magnificent revolutionary worker."

"You should watch the documentary about the Chauvet Cave.
It puts things into perspective."
"Chaumet has a cave?"

"Sublime! The cardigans were an aneurysm!"

"He came out at the end of the fashion show,
but it was a formality, he didn't do anything . . ."

"You have to shock them. Not intimidate them.
Nuance . . ."

"Marketing has split us up into two teams:
the formal content team and the emotional content team."

"I pay her $35,000 a day;
it would be nice if she arrived on time."

"The magazine layout turned out brilliantly.
Sales will collapse."

"She said my dress isn't modern,
and they canceled it.
I've been working on it since December."

"I'm dying!"
(about shoes)

"Camille is coming!"
"Camille? Camille who?"
"Kanye."

"No, I don't like it. It's not modern."

"He told me, 'Hello, I'm the CEO of Gucci,
but whatever I do in my life,
Gucci will always be bigger than me.'"

"He's too radical. He can't express himself
with words. So he makes dresses."

"She's already seventeen. Getting old . . .
She was beautiful, though . . ."

"The day before the collection, he arrives
and destroys everything. It's great,
it brings immediacy and urgency."

"I'll beat the next person
who says the word *modern*."

"It's a full moon and the city is full of models.
How do you expect me to sleep?"

"What I'm expecting is a collection
that will destroy my wardrobe
and make me look like a yokel
with only thirty-five walks on the runway."

"In an attempt to be nice, I think she eats
newborn kittens for breakfast."

"She eats at Café de Flore.
It makes her feel like she's reading."

"He's on fire. With him, World War One
would have lasted two years."

"What day is it?"

"Is your perfume in the top ten?"
"Yes."
"I've never smelled it."
"Oh, yes, you have. It's the smell of taxis."

"Come on, a Kate Moss menu for everyone!"
"You mean, nothing?"

"OK, you can film her from the front
but from a distance. Left profile is OK;
right profile is not.
Most importantly, never from behind. OK?"

"When Americans say someone
is mean, it's a mark of respect
and admiration."

"No, that looks too literally like a billionaire.
It's not modern."

"Her job is to make sure that we don't give
the same dress to two celebrities.
You can't imagine the pressure.
She's losing her hair."

"OK. I'm going to get rude
but it's not personal.
It's because this is war.
It will only last till Wednesday, though. OK?"

"Her brain is wearing pink, low-cut pants."

"I don't tell my mom about the castings anymore
because it breaks her heart
when I'm not taken, and now with this pimple
on my forehead . . ."

"Was it beautiful?"
"Yes, beautiful, but completely off the mark."

"Fashion is weirder than fiction."

"Be careful, you have your press tag
hanging on your jacket."

"I don't understand. When you say
'this is asylum,' is that a good thing or a bad thing?"

"The assistants are so young.
At lunch they were eating Gerber
in the kitchen."

"They paid for forty pages of ads this year,
so I don't see how we can write less than 2,000 words on them.
Oh well, just spread it out . . ."

"I'm waiting for the designer
who will take a selfie while greeting the audience."

"Did you sleep? Lucky you."

"Girls! Show the bag better!
No one buys a bag they can't see."

"Stop posing like Tom Ford,
with your eyebrows all furrowed
like you want to fuck the whole world."

"Last season we had
our best couture sales in twenty-two years.
Do you want champagne again?"

"When she's not moving, she's pretty ugly.
But when she walks, she looks amazing."
"She's a beast."

"Her name is Camilla. But with a *K*
and only one *L*. Kamila."

"Yes, that's the backstage TV badge,
but you won't be able to film.
You need another badge for that."

"Put the burgundy bag on her;
it's more modern."

"Swarovski is like chicken,
you can never get enough."

"Give her a smokey eye but natural."

"It's a beige red."

"During couture, the Four Seasons
is full of princesses who have yet to be overthrown."

"It's absurd, but absurdity
is our business."

"Two years ago it was shocking,
but now we're in a post-Miley world."

"My driver just declared his love to me.
I have to stop seducing everyone."

"Coming from her, sublime means lousy."

"I can't take it anymore.
Tonight, it's the Versace show,
a snack, and then straight to bed."

"Don't even talk about it; I love art!"

"I know there are people dying in the world,
but let's fix one problem at a time,
starting with your hair."

"She's American, but she's smart."

"The collection was so ugly
that going up to give her a kiss at the end was a nightmare.
I have to go take a shower."

"She has perfect skin.
In the end, cruelty keeps you young."

"It was divisive."
"You mean, atrocious?"
"Yes."

"If I'm the sincerest out of all of his friends,
he's in trouble."

"I slept three hours last night.
I'm alive again."

"I remember the fashion show she did
with the uneven heels. The girls were limping.
It was so moving."

"He speaks at the funerals of his collaborators.
If I die before retirement, I will be entitled
to my own phallocratic eulogy."

"Our customers are so prehistoric,
they draw bison on the walls of the store."

"The nude pink, yes.
The piglet pink, no."

"He forced us to listen to the same
Tina Turner album for seventy-two hours of fittings."

"My babysitter taught my daughter
that Lindsay Lohan is the Big Bad Wolf."

"After a sleepless night in the workshop,
we turn off the heat in the morning.
It wakes the interns up."

"Holy crinoline."

"This pair of boots costs $100,000.
They are couture."

"The inspiration is Joan of Arc in Miami."

"Frankly, I have never received such a beautiful gift!
And I once got a Hermès hammock . . ."

"Her name is Anne-Marie but without a dash or an *E*.
Annmari."

"Her name is Ine.
Like Inès but without the *S*."

"Next!"
(to a model, before she finishes the casting demo steps)

"I've never had plastic surgery.
Never. Except my nose."

"It was couture sport,
$150,000 for the sweatpants."

"Rumor has it that he started taking selfies."

"My armpits smell weird.
I think I'm sweating champagne."

"Can you give me some gum?
I have 1992 fall/winter breath."

"Have you seen Mouna Ayoub's boots?
They're basically two yachts."

"I don't know when it was.
I'm confusing Sunday evening and this morning."

"It's an invisible red."

"No, I had to sell the Park Avenue apartment.
I didn't get phone reception there."

"As much as last year was the year of the eye,
this year is the year of the lip."

"Yes! Nike haute couture!"

"They want to make a reality show about me,
but not vulgar, you know?"

"Wait, I'm going to get a glass of water to drink."
"You're right! Vitamins . . ."

"I met him three biennials ago."

"My driver has clipper marks on the back of his neck."

"We have special jewelry orders.
Russians wanting skulls designed
with ruby blood coming out of their mouths."

"She thinks she's in a David Lynch movie,
but she's in a Tarantino."

"Her husband made his fortune through Frisbee."

"The bum down my street has an iPhone."

"She's a perfume hotshot.
She has a whole network of noses."

"Take the neon-pink power strip off the makeup table.
I really have to tell you everything."
"You really are lame."
(from a designer to a world-famous makeup artist)

"That's him in the back. Behind the guy
with the Dior suit from spring 2011.
Or winter 2012? I can't remember . . ."

"Do you plan on playing music that's long enough
if the standing ovation lasts for ten minutes?
You never know."

"No worries.
I'll drink five espressos, and I'll be fine."

"I was reading her email and I didn't understand
why she was talking about Russian socialists.
I had read it wrong. Russian socialites."

"I was sitting between a conservative writer and a blogger."

"Are you OK? Isn't your brain too divided?"

"They called us in for a meeting to demand less
artistry in our artistic direction.
At least that was clear."

"From now on, general bathroom ban,
everyone on deck."

"Models look fat in it.
So imagine real people . . ."

"She bought the Chanel guillotine by Tom Sachs.
She installed it in her entranceway in Venice.
It looks likes a foundation, for sure."

"The inspiration was supersonic Sagan in space."

"No one reads us anymore,
apart from the advertisers, and they only
go through with a ruler
to quantify their return on advertising."

"I don't want hipsters. They buy
two T-shirts and leave two seconds later,
after destroying your image."

"His first collection was all garbage bags. Great."

"Today he's adorable. We're all terrified."

"My intern was born last year.
Like he doesn't know who Carla Bruni is.
It's refreshing, and you save time in the end."

"Oh shit, stairs . . ."
(said while wearing 7-inch heels)

"She conveys stress really well.
She would make a really good press agent for stress."

"Then again, I understand.
Who would be normal in her position?"

"He sells youth.
All of my dermatologist friends buy his clothes."

"We don't sell clothes; we sell thrills."

"He's a hair guru."

"Her maternity ward selfies were terrible.
But it's getting better since she started to shed."

"Are you coming to CK?"
"There's a Calvin Klein party?"
"No, Caviar Kaspia for drinks, silly."

"Thanks, but I do not wear prototypes."
(note attached to a fur coat returned to a designer)

"No more jet-skiing in Saint-Barth!
My daughter is hellbent on
calculating the family's carbon footprint.
She's a green dictator."

"You can't write that it's unwearable,
so we say it was 'an interesting gamble.'
Readers get it."

"I don't think you realize
the magnitude of what I'm going through."

"I'm at the end of my fashion rope."

"How do I tell him it wasn't great?"
"Tell him it was really beautiful.
He'll understand."

"I came home unexpectedly, and
my boyfriend was eating chips."

"No. You can't stream a broadcast
of the fashion show.
Couture is not streamable, darling."

"When Stalin died, it took his freaked-out assistant
five days to get into the room.
For her, we'll wait until she's decomposed."

"You can never have too much champagne when it's free."

"Yes, visually it's striking,
but in real life this woman
reeks of perfume."

"I know, now when you say Samuel Beckett
people think of Gucci first,
but he was a great playwright, too."

"Is this Le Bon Marché?"
(said in front of the Musée d'Orsay)

"How many renovations has she done on her face?"
"As many as the number of paint coats on the Eiffel Tower."

"The inspiration was a rave set in the Renaissance."

"This scented candle smells like
the girdle of an old Swiss lady."

"They organized a cocktail party
at the Paris Aquarium and served sushi.
It was a little redundant."

"He turns everything into flattery.
Once he told me that
my failures were inspiring."

"Fashion people! We love them all . . ."
"-ish!"

"It's art director Alex Liberman's
golden rule: When a photo is ugly, print it huge.
Huge makes everything better."

"Never admit that you've cheated on him,
or that it's Zara."

"It was perfect.
But it was nothing."

"We made a special dressing room for the designer
backstage. It looks like the *Evil Dead* house."

"The fashion show was about to begin, and my editor in chief
is yelling, 'Give me a tweet, quick.'
I gave her a joke that only got three retweets.
She's going to fire me."

"I love your bag. I have the same one in mauve,
in green, in blue, in black varnish, and
in two-tone red and green."

"When the fashion shows are over, do you think
Anna eats spaghetti carbonara in gray sweats?"

"It's a painting by Ferdinand Léger."

"I was doing a session with Kate Moss
and Helmut Newton at the San Regis in Paris.
I walk in and Helmut tells me . . ."
(an anecdote that starts off well)

"I was with these people and everything was shining.
Their hair, their clothes, their swimming pool.
Everything was shining except their eyes."

"After 10 PM he sits down in front of his Banksy,
and he smokes without saying anything."

"I don't know what real life is.
I've never bought anything, never worked,
never paid for anything."

"I hate pleasantries. Having said that,
I do them very well. With a bottle
of white wine, I can talk to an empty chair."

"Let's face it: Basically, I don't do shit."

"American women are anti-appeal, made of plastic.
They love family, children. It's anti femme fatale."

"The real truth is, I'm on another planet."

"Weren't you in the Paris-Milan fashion
cattle car at 9:35 this morning?"

"Her parents called her Binx because when she was a baby
she looked like Jar Jar Binks from *Star Wars*."

"She's not just a hairdresser.
She is the Meryl Streep of hair.
She has reinvented me a hundred times."

"In one night we repainted all of our two hundred stores
white so that you can only
see the product. Sales have exploded."

"I'm descaling my assistant."

"I am a digital curator."

"Good job, you really have lost weight!"
"Yes, I was sick . . ."
"Congratulations!"

"Her name is Liisa. With two *I*s."

"More is more is more is more."

"She looks like Jayne Mansfield
but beheaded."

"My mother had no friends whatsoever.
She used to go to old people's funerals,
because they were the only places she could get in
without an invitation."

"I overdid it with the bleaching.
I have luminescent teeth. When I open my mouth
in my sleep, it wakes my boyfriend up."

"It's subversive glamour."
(about Prada)

"She's so 1.0 I bet she only charges her phone every other day."

"She could drive down the Champs-Élysées
in a taxi without looking up from her phone."

"I can't invite you, we're in a tight space.
The fashion show takes place in a womb of two hundred people."

"I'm rusty like a
1968 Paco Rabanne dress."

"We need to talk to each other soon."
"OK, I'm setting an alarm."

"This music . . . feels like
we're in a Polish brothel."

"Perfection is the end of everything."

"You dress any old way,
it's not editable at all."

"She runs on a loop.
She's basically in monogossip."

"Sorry I put you in the second row,
but I have so many celebrities
that my first row ended up in second row."

"My driver is culture-free."

"I found my son an internship in Milan.
He came back with a fake tan and his eyebrows plucked.
Thank you, Italy."

"You don't say *predictable*, you say *perfect*."

"It's a Nutella dress: regressive,
bad for your figure,
but no one can resist it."

"It's about to begin! You, go plug up the holes
in the first row with stand-ins
who have pretty faces."

"Looks like a vacuumed panther."
(about their boss two rows in front of them)

"No, we can't film him getting off the jet.
He's 'for the people,'
and he has to keep that image."

"I feel like I'm talking into nothingness all day long, all the time,
and the only concrete thing is my Celine bag."

"My background is in contemporary art,
so this is just playtime for me.
You all are so cute."

"Four hours a night for ten days,
but my calligrapher gave me
Quinton Hypertonic, so that keeps me going."

"Oranges are very Jacquemus.
Cupcakes are not Jacquemus."

"She opened the Calvin show."
(looking distraught)

"Naked, he must be sexy, but he dresses so badly.
You really have to imagine the onion after it's peeled . . ."

"It was . . . commercial."

"His best friend told me everything,
how much of a douche he actually is."

"Do you want to see the dessert menu?"
(they burst out in genuine laughter)

"She has four assistants. But basically
the whole world is her assistant."

"I congratulated her on her magazine
and she told me that she was fired.
Why was I not aware of this, and
why are we still inviting her?"

"She has the body of a Louis XV pedestal table."
"But the vocabulary of an Ikea shelf."

"She ages gracefully.
Celinity and senility."

"She's so smart, it's ridiculous."

"It's a sculpture by Daniel Craig."
(pointing to a Tony Cragg sculpture in the entrance
to the Fendi store on Avenue Montaigne)

"He pushes the fabric to its limits."

"You don't say *rigid material*, you say *armor*.
You don't say *botched*, you say *wild*.
You don't say *flashy*, you say *sensual*."

"They say he's straight."

"It was OK, but I didn't feel its importance
deep in my soul either."

"She works at Hermès."
(dreamy silence)

"Did you sleep with him?"
"No, we just went to the movies together
to see *Blue Is the Warmest Color*."
"It's like you've slept together, isn't it?"

"She is a Saint Laurent sovereigntist.
She is stuck in the Russian ballets collection.
Everything else is just Crocs to her."

"Is that smoke I smell?"
"Yes, it's my ass."

"Don't leave your jacket lying around like that . . ."
"It's from last season. Nobody is going to steal it."

"The briefing for the models was
'chic but upbeat nonetheless.'"

"I went to her house. She makes you drink
from glasses that were Colette
scented candles. The water tastes like fig."

"I'm more creative than what you see
in the magazine. They utilize eight percent of me."
"And that's great."
"So imagine if I was really working."

"We did a study: Clients hate it
but it puts the brand back on a pedestal
of positive snobbery for our selective circle."

"He is uncompromising on everything.
Even his briefs are uncompromising."

"She J'adores everything."

"If only we could erase
her last five collections from our
collective memory."

"Your hairstyle is still
a bit too improvisational."

"She's not isosceles."

"My dream was to smoke opium
with Betty Catroux but my daughter wanted
me to bring her back a selfie with Cara . . ."

"I met him at the Etam dinner
at the Brasserie Lipp."

"He's my oldest friend.
We've known each other for three years."

"When was yesterday?"

"I heard she makes placenta smoothies,
and I have to admit it suits her."

"He can't help but redo everything over and over again.
So we pay him to take a vacation
so that he's only there fifteen days before the fashion show."

"Is your dress inside out?"
"No, it's Rodarte."

"If you describe the collection as it is,
you'll lose exclusives for ten years . . ."
"I'll just describe the celebrities in the front row."

"It is a houndsfoot print."

"He really renewed the value of fun in luxury."

"You don't understand, I'm at odds with objects."
(to explain her new but already butchered Valentino bag)

"Oh look, it's Beyoncé!"
(in front of Rihanna at the exit of Balmain)

"I'm an e-influence administrator."

"It was sublime.
I had a beauty seizure."

"Don't format your emails and edit out mistakes,
or people will think you have time for that sort of thing.
If it's a mess, they'll think you're overwhelmed."

"We have to give her flowers.
It's a pain in the ass."
"Then buy her some stinky flowers."

"I'm so happy, my daughter has de-Kardashianized."

"Never too much."

"I live in upper Manhattan."
"You mean Washington Heights?"

"Can you imagine having so much power?"
(talking about an influencer)

"I'm naturally on E."

"Oh, no thanks, I don't read."
(to the girl handing out magazines)

"Inspiration? There isn't any.
The inspiration is the crazy schedule
and a deadline."

"We're done with the patent-leather minidress.
We thought about the atrocious girl who would buy it
and if we really wanted to feed that beast."

"They announced their profits are over fifty percent."
"Not hard, they just have to sell two bags per season."
"They must have sold three of those and POW."

"I'm exhausted.
You put me next to a Picasso painting,
and you can only tell the difference between Dora Maar and me
because she has a golden frame."

"I'm dead . . ."
"Yes, it shows."

"He is so sure of himself that his
business plan includes
a revenue stream from the lawsuits
he thinks he'll win against the counterfeiters."

"Waking up is hard.
But after 5 PM it gets easier."

"This is hell. Have you seen hell?
Well, this is hell."

"How many circles are there in hell?
We just passed through the ninth circle of hell,
so I'm asking how many are left."

"It was the Last Judgment.
I was hiding in a Vuitton store,
and the walls were screaming,
'She's here! Come and take her!'"

"He's organizing tomorrow's Kate Moss party,
but it's going to be too small, so tonight
he knocked down the loadbearing walls."

"My daughter is fifteen years old. When I leave her somewhere,
I'm afraid the cops will blow her up,
because she looks just like an abandoned package."

"She's wearing Celine, circa pre–Phoebe Philo."

"It's a timeless line,
But starting from today."

"Slow down, you're going to crush forty bloggers."
(exiting the Dior fashion show)

"I listened to the news on the radio in the car
between fashion shows. It's horrible outside."

"She had to move."
"Why? Did her head not fit through the door anymore?"

"She gets bored very quickly. Never speak to her for more
than thirty seconds."

"We hit rock bottom twenty years ago.
Now we're cleaning up the cracks."

"She is inspiring. You look at her,
and you get a hundred ideas."

"He looked prettier when he had a neck."

"She bombarded me with sexts.
What part of *gay* doesn't she understand?"

"It's Friday. I feel like Monday
is a month away."

"Congratulations, it took me ten minutes of flipping through
your magazine before I came across
the first article because of all the advertising."

"She lives in the suburbs."
(index finger like a gun against the temple)

"I thought it was the end of the world
because the clouds were so dark.
But it was just the tinted windows of the car."

"The catwalk was super long.
Poor models. I got blisters on my eyes just looking at them."

"He's so corrupt . . . And I'm the one
saying it, so you can imagine!"

"I live in a 350-square-foot apartment, but
my necklace is worth a thousand square feet."

"We don't say *surgeon* anymore,
we say *epidermisologist*
or *filler doctor*."

"A TV cameraman asked me
what I thought of the horrible announcer at the fashion show . . .
Someone took a bead on my forehead."

"I was in the first row at Dior today.
It took me fifteen years to get it. I was touched."

"We had to redo all of our stores in China."
"Redecorate?"
"No. Move. We had the wrong neighborhoods."

"It was so awful leaving my still-in-bed boyfriend's
chocolate-croissant aroma
for my driver's industrial grapefruit musk . . ."

"I came by subway.
At 42nd Street there was a guy playing
Michael Jackson's 'Heal the World' on sax."

"The inspiration is an Middle-Eastern billionaire,
but not flashy."

"I don't care about beauty.
I want truth."

"She only wears things not yet in stores."

"She is perpetually fired up.
She has a master's degree in drama."

"It's beautiful from the front,
but from the back it's hideous."

"Poor thing, she looks like a patchwork
of trash cans, and it cost her a fortune."

"We're a hit! I just ordered 19,000 zippers."

"He spends so much time in rehab,
I don't know when he has time to take drugs."

"No, but her skin is orange.
Doesn't she realize that?
Does her mirror not have colors?"

"It was awful. If my assistant tells me
that she loved it, I'm firing her."

"Oh shit, they sat us in the hyenas' section."
"Where do you see the doves' section?"

"Come on, let's go to the next fashion show
that will contradict this one."

"Don't eat. You'll have to digest,
and that's exhausting."

"It's the improbable shoe contest."

"I'm deciding between siccing my lawyer on him
or my shrink."

"Are you wide awake?"
"I would be if I had slept."

"He was a contestant on season one of *Beauty and the Geeks,*
but not on the team of beauties."

"It's the Diet Coke of creation."

"It's rilly modeurne."

"It's an intestinal war."

"We used to take inspirational trips
to Mongolia and loot secondhand-clothing stores.
Now we're stuck with Tumblr."

"The turnover has increased tenfold,
and the flower budget has dropped tenfold."

"I'm so drunk, I could tweet the truth."

"If their sellers are paid on commission,
they're going to be eating Top Ramen all winter."

"He made a fortune selling horrors
to rich people who were convinced they were buying
beauty. He's the Bernie Madoff of the puffer jacket."

"OK, you can do the interview,
but just one question."

"When's the Kate Moss party already?"
"Last night."

"She sat me down in Siberia."

"Are you taking the extensions off the model?"
(looking at the hair on the floor)
"No, she's losing her hair."

"The inspiration is the madness of humanity,
our common fear, and
the feeling of going beyond common sense."

"My feet are sleepy."

"It was powerful, classic, nice, smart.
It made me depressed."

"Oh dear, I want to read a book."

"It's a Givenchy prototype from three seasons ago.
It's practically a museum piece. Feels like
being at a Met Museum fashion exhibition."

"Make the foundation really light,
and take off the lips."

"As soon as she says something to you,
she sends a recap email to protect herself:
'I'm going to the bakery.' With fifteen people cc'ed."

"She can never be editor in chief.
She is out of control. Once she wore
a Chanel bag to a Dior fashion show."

"No way, no interview, but you can go congratulate him."

"I remember exactly what I was doing when I heard
that Marc Jacobs was leaving Vuitton."

"She's cultivated, a bit hard and cold;
this girl is the Palais de Tokyo."

"He wrote Cartier as 'Quartier' in an email.
He blamed autocorrect,
but I'm spreading the rumor anyway."

"Listening to him talk is like trying
to read a script that has random pages torn out."

"I came back from Dries Van Noten
and wanted to redo everything at home.
But like my man says:
'No decisions during fashion week.'"

"He met him on Grindr, but it's cute anyway."

"She was in Los Angeles,
so we did the fittings on FaceTime.
It was easier."

"Welcome to the best-dressed mental asylum in the world."

"I went to the Louvre yesterday before Chloé.
The yellow wall behind the *Mona Lisa*,
can anyone explain it to me?
This country needs an artistic director."

"Smile, but with your eyes.
With teeth, it's silly."

"I was sitting across from Rihanna,
so I didn't see anything at the fashion show."

"He couldn't go to the Stella McCartney fashion show.
He is in a fetal position in his bed
at the Meurice; he can't take it anymore."

"She is a leather-goods manager.
This winter she was out sick for a month.
I think a thousand crocodiles were spared."

"She's been doing all the fashion shows
since New York, so a whole month, eating only
sweeteners. Respect."

"Ah, is that all?"
(after waiting an hour to see a flash fashion show)

"We're working on the social teasers for the event."

"I have blockbuster gossip. Want to hear it?"

"She has the uninhibited charm of vulgar people."

"So? Resting, are we?"
(at 3 AM, to an intern who was taking an Instagram break)

"There is a hipster-phobia movement
that was launched by yuppies.
Talk about a fight."

"I'm at the Grand Palais while they're setting up
for Chanel tomorrow.
It's so crazy,
I can't talk anymore, I'll call you back."

"I preferred without a mouth."
"I don't like mouths that are too mouthy.
Especially since she has a lot of eyes."
"We moisturize and that's it."

"Who is that?"
(pointing to Kate Moss)

"I wanted to get a tattoo, but
with the hustle and bustle of the fashion shows,
it would get infected."

"You haven't met the right straight guys, that's all."

"What do you want to drink?"
"A Coke Zero, please."
"And you?"
"Do you have Coke Thousand?"

"I was next to Rihanna at Dior.
Her fur reeked like weed.
I was high by the end of the fashion show."

"We're going to recontextualize the flagship."

"I dreamed that we put Anna Wintour
in the standing section."
"Don't say that kind of stuff out loud.
You'll end up institutionalized."

"Her name is Cécilia. But it's pronounced Tchitchilia."

"In Courchevel, there are no more creperies,
only Vuitton stores. I ate fondue next to a woman
in a Chanel one-shoulder dress."

"He touches your head, and it's a journey
in your body."

"It's a leather race. I saw the guy
from a large luxury group buy ten thousand
calves from Aveyron, right in front of me."

"She gets eccentricity and lack of hygiene mixed up."

"These are $800 pants.
They're a response to customer demand
for more exclusive pants."

"You know the 'easy open' label
on boxes of pasta?
She's got the same on her jeans."

"Her résumé is amazing, but they all want to work
in luxury. He could have run the Louvre,
but he'd rather run a store."

"Oh my, I got goose bumps."
(in front of Dr. Martens covered with big rhinestones)

"I have nothing else to wear.
I'm going to end up in a cellar . . . alone."

"She's got breasts, that's the problem."

"I've slept for a total of four hours this month."

"Even the phrase 'out of sync' is too out of sync to describe
what we're going through."

"It's a new morning.
An important morning."

"My excitometer reached seven billion."

"We live in the cold and the crowds,
like in the elevator of the Eiffel Tower.
We're complaining, but we're in the heart
of the Eiffel Tower."

"I have reverse tastes: When I'm on a perfume shoot
and I think the campaign hideous,
the perfume is a success."

"He became a millionaire with his charity business in Asia."

"It's functional. It's ready-to-wear
ready to go."

"I produced a movie.
It's Marina Abramović, naked. In 3-D."
"Were the spectators as afraid as
in front of *L'arrivée d'un train en gare de La Ciotat*?"

"Can we do the interview?"
"Yes, I gave you a four-minute slot in two hours."

"There were too many people in the front row.
She was crushed. Anna put herself
in the second row. It was Pompeii."

"Do what you want.
It's just that Jackie Kennedy wouldn't have done that."

"VIP lounges are so *Roseanne*."

"Well, Chanel has done it before, but if we don't do
what Chanel has already done,
we won't do anything anymore, right?"
"Nothing! Nothing!"

"She wears any old thing she wants,
but since she has the authority of the boss, it works."

"It's so 'young designer' that it's like
being dressed in artisanal feta."

"You think maybe it isn't so terrible?
Wait until tomorrow, when it's all over
and she gazes out into the void in front of her.
I'd rather not be here for that."

"It was beautiful, very elementary.
A beauty that can become ugly in its beauty."

"Even Barbès got really gentrified."

"I saw them kissing backstage at Chanel.
They crushed us with their love."

"He has power, so he's lost."

"I'm going to the Vuitton party. Do you want me to get
some dirt after people get drunk?"

"It was an iconic font for two to three days."

"I look like the undead."
"Which means you don't look bougie, so it's OK."

"I was feeling pretty good for the first ten minutes
after my shower."

"Gérard Bovary, it's me."

"She needs to stop annoying me
with her caviar problems."

"We're looking for a plain
beauty editor to add weight
to the beauty content."

"So you got a new tattoo?"
"Yes. Mountains. Simple."

"I try to make clothes that are timeless
but at the same time very for this time."

"What we are trying to develop
is a really powerful seven seconds of content
for our Instagram."

"He's such a bad photographer.
In his pictures of Florence, Michelangelo's *David*
looks like a fat lump."

"He reminds me of Grenouille
in the movie *Perfume*, but without the smell."

"We did a crease at the knee of the pants,
which allows you to curl into the fetal position."

"Traveling is horrible . . .
Rio next week, I can't take any more."

"She was in Abercrombie.
I was in Dries Van Noten.
And she wants to teach me lessons?"

"I'm not asking for much.
If I can cry at the end of an episode,
I'm happy."

"Aren't they weird, those faded jeans
that make you look like
you've just pissed bleach?"

"I made you huge gluten-free pizzas."

"I'm not going to do the cultural stuff
on my weekend in Las Vegas."
"Cultural?"
"The Grand Canyon."
"Oh, the Grand Canyon sucks."

"Three months ago she was the stylist
who gave orders to the world,
and now she talks to herself on the metro platform."

"Apart from the Russian twins
and the country boy, I haven't kissed anyone.
I'm in a desert. I feel ugly."

"It's like he took steroids
but it backfired."

"She walks with her shoulder pulled back like
Karen Elson used to.
It looks like she's walking sitting down."

"If you look at it in terms of the history
of the garment, slim just keeps
getting slimmer."

"He takes pictures for the fanzine *Crush*."
"Model or photographer?"
"Both. He takes selfies for them."

"In New York, everything is so tall.
When you come back to Paris everything looks flat.
You feel like you're living in a crepe."

"I was at that crazy dinner last night.
We weren't allowed to use Instagram
or Twitter. I can't tell you anything,
but it was crazy."

"She built a villa for herself near Monaco.
In the plans, it looked magnificent, but in real life
it looks like a Leonard Cohen song."

"I just ate a $45 egg
at Prunier. I have to debrief you."

"I have an advertiser's cocktail party tonight.
It's going to be a blowjob festival."

"Ah, the trip to Venice . . .
I spent the whole thing popping Xanax."

"Where did it happen?"
"No idea. It was six months ago,
and I erase my mental hard drive every season,
otherwise it's madness, you know?"

"He's hungry. Like we're all gonna end up
in his stomach."

"She's killing the magazine
with her expense reports.
Prada expense report after Prada expense report;
she's killing us."

"My daughter took emojis as her main language."

"Woof! You're sexy!"
"It's nice of you to say that,
but I look like an omelet with hair."

"We need to save her from herself.
I'm talking about a global system reboot."

"You give her the choice between two photos,
a beautiful one and an ugly one,
and you can bet that she'll stick the ugly one on the cover."

"And what do you do?"
"I'm in the inspiration business."

"I had to list my hobbies at the end of my CV,
but you can't write 'depression, American Apparel, and Le Bain,'
so I put tennis."

"You're more likely to die in a chairlift accident with Shakira
than win Mega Millions. But go ahead, play."

"My mom was looking at a photo of a puppy on my phone.
She swiped over to the next photo.
She won't be able to call me 'sweetie' anymore."

"She's thinks she looks like Charlize Theron,
but she looks more like the J'adore bottle."

"My daughter is watching *The Little Mermaid,*
but muted with Miley Cyrus playing over it.
A beautiful bipolarity is brewing here."

"It's Sunday at 11 PM, but instead can we just
say we skipped the week so it's Friday at 5 PM
and the weather is nice and JFK Jr. isn't dead?"

"He's posting so many selfies on Instagram
that if scroll through his timeline fast enough, it comes alive
and you can see the duckface moving."

"It is an atypical space in the Bronx,
but with a timeless view."

"My neighbor's boyfriend is called
OhMartinOhMartinOhMartin,
and he's loudly trying to fix the bed."

"My mom is so shy.
In virtual life she would have been lame.
She would have poked my dad for two years.
I wouldn't have been born."

"She's a Southern girl with a feminist twist."

"Nine percent of my brain is occupied
with phone-battery anxiety.
Where am I at? Should the screen brightness
be lowered? When do I need to find an outlet?"

"My autocorrect puts in *orgy*
instead of *Orly*. I've just called in
the whole film crew for an orgy."

"For the clothing in the show, we have the budget
they had for the opening title on *Lost*."

"How long is the probation period for the interns?"
"Three minutes."

"She has a very sample sales silhouette,
but she is quite chic, yes."

"Her mother was the kind of Parisian
who really has style but no soul.
She inherited nothing except for the
1,300-square-foot apartment on Trocadero."

"She has that hypocritical nanny's high-pitched voice."

"In my company,
if you look rested you're suspicious."

"Now she has her November body,
but as soon as she stops eating 130 cookies a day,
she gets her July body back in a week."

"She scraped her beige Birkin on the first day.
World War Three."

"My father is so Floridian.
He just picked up a white iPhone."

"She has more bags than books.
And friends."

"I am a cosmetics storyteller.
Beauty, all that."

"For his CV, in terms of education
let's say he has a Google MFA."

"The advantage for recent migrants
is that they think the weather is normal."

"He writes with an alert
and vivid copy/paste."

"Since the divorce, my father has
stopped caring. Monday morning he came
home with a huge hickey
shaped like a Porsche Cayenne."

"He was found dead on his bed.
Hand in a bag of chips."

"She has the charm of the automated voice that
makes announcements on the subway platform."

"How do you translate *spiritualité?*"

"He's manly. He can imitate the sound of a Peugeot."

"We've seen Donald Judds that can reconcile you
with Donald Judd."

"It's a capsule collection with ten percent
of the proceeds going to charity.
You do yourself good, and you do good."

"He said *abdomen*. I can't date someone who says *abdomen*."

"This morning I went into a trance when I saw
a flower on the wisteria. I feel old."

"I took the train. The collapse . . .
it's like the Isabel Marant clearance sale
but without the clothes."

"She never turns off the heat all year round.
In the hot months, she opens the window.
She has a hundred miles
of melted glaciers on her conscience."

"You know how you can make people
yawn by yawning in front of them?
Well, she has that power,
but she doesn't have to yawn in front of you."

"Did you have sex on vacation in New York?"
"No, there were only Americans."

"We got a CV from the perfect
kid with multiple degrees. We call him, and his voicemail says:
'Cooeehomies, leave a message after the fart.'"

"So, how was your hookup?"
"I got to his place, and he had an electric blanket.
Orgasming was impossible."

"You don't say *navy blue*, you say she worked on
an *industrial tar*."

"Tel Aviv is my Brittany."

"Oh no, I stopped tweeting the stupid things I heard.
It was too time-consuming."

"The country folks are the ones
who are the devils."

"Their party was called 'Fuck Me, I'm Famous.'
Yes."

"Fashion is over.
People have moved on."

"You talk to him too much.
He sees you like you're under the crude
fluorescent lights of a laundromat.
No mystery. You've got to subdue."

"My daughter talks about her math teacher's ass
with lecherous eyes."

"But . . . did you pay for those shoes?"

"I would like a black carrot juice, please."

"I hate any change. I'm neophobic."

"My son thinks death
is two reality TV contestants
holding hands before they know
who is eliminated."

"Four-ear headphones,
that's real romance."

"You had breakfast, right?"
"Yes, I just ate two acres of cereal."

"I was so high on ecstasy at the Gaultier tattoos fashion show
in 1994 that I couldn't see anything.
I held the microphone up to the vibrations."

"It's a dishonest dress."

"Oh, I love those white sneakers.
Oh man, they're price-on-request."

"When he speaks, I hear the sound of mistakes."

"He does arthouse fashion.
These are auteur shirts."

"These are philosophy books
for the subway. In ten stations
we'll teach you the Derrida & Co.
at a really nice price."

"He's awful but we can't hold that against him
when you look at the bags he comes up with
season after season."

"If a bombshell explodes in the middle of this dinner
there won't be any more fashion in Paris."
"Uh, no, there will only be forty less snobs."

"You know the adage that
you should never make an ugly dress
because someone is going to buy it?
Well, that also goes for bags."

"Since there are a dozen of us
going on this picnic, I suggest
that we pick the hashtag right away
for social media consistency."

"What's your bag? A thermal bag?"

"She's so alter-globalization
that she fell asleep
during *The Wolf of Wall Street*."

"She's condescendering."

"She's really, really mean.
The editorial staff calls her Loubutin.
Louboutin Putin."

"If you don't like spoilers,
don't look at your boyfriend's
father's body."

"Remember when we did the water park
slides on Molly?
Well, this morning is the exact opposite."

"Yeah, but she has a very healthy,
constructive violence."

"She wears some old stuff.
I imagine she's waiting for it to come back on trend."

"For breakfast, I eat a lemon herbal tea
and I'm full."

"Be reminded that we are masstige digital experts."

"As soon as he opens his mouth to speak,
time slows and you feel like
you're riding the entire A line on the subway."

"If we gave her a dollar every time
she tweeted something mean,
she could wear Saint Laurent head to toe."

"In meetings eight out of ten of us wear Stan Smiths."
"Did you notice that the highest paid people
wear the most worn out ones?"

"She talks to me about ecology
with her three televisions, her subscription
to a thousand channels, her two cars,
and her lousy blonde dye job."

"I'm in the country. Countryside.
Everything smells of cumin. I tell you,
it's really real. . ."

"When I left Paris for the country,
it was a shock—as much for them as for me.
I wore Rick Owens to go to the bakery. Once."

"I reread *The Devil Wears Prada*.
It got old. Young people are worse today.
The devil wears Mango."

"You reread *The Devil Wears Prada*?
Seriously?"

"Do you want champagne?"
"No, thank you, that reminds me too much of work."

"You know me, I'm happy if I fuck or work."

"Don't even suggest giving her a tour.
If there is no escalator,
she's not going to your beach."

"We have a reality TV project
about the flea market."

"Damn the claustrophobic atmosphere . . ."
(looking at a tree)

"The nearest APC store is two time zones away."

"Why is that bird banging on the glass?"
"He thinks his reflection is a male rival."

"He Cavallizes everything. On him,
Hermès looks flashy."

"He's a living PSA against beer."

"The stupid financier came over and said,
'Sky's the limit,' knowing that we are
working in a basement where the sky
is four inches over our heads."

"He lives in another dimension.
The Labor Day dimension. He doesn't do shit."

"I got my press card."
"Seriously???"

"She's a TV-realitress."

"We put a sun-kiss effect on the bridge of her nose."

"Her tan is beyond Pantone.
Compared to her, Valentino is pale."

"I'm a tattoo stylist."

"More than a coach, he's a body engineer, you know."

"Hello, do you have
the *New York Times* from yesterday?"

"Yes, but it's a tongue-in-cheek selfie."

"I'm warning you, this Saturday night
I'm living like there is no Sunday."

"He is not beautiful, but he lives like he's beautiful."

"I'm the shoe manager."

"She rents a dressing room
at the H&M on Rivoli."

"I'm a press agent—I don't even know
when I'm lying anymore."
"Tell me about it. I'm a journalist; it's even worse."

"It reminds me of the day the CEO
discovered the flower budget
for the muse . . ."

"I have Jerusalem/Saint-Tropez syndrome.
I oscillate between the two."

"Have you ever done a casting in Milan?
That is brutal. Italians make you regret being born.
In the end, you apologize for having a face."

"Nicolas Ghesquière just Instagrammed
his Stan Smiths shoes with his face on the tongue.
I'm so jealous."

"She takes so many cigarette breaks,
she looks like a caryatid outside the office."

"Sir, you're hurting Paris!"
(slamming the cab door)

"She has monochrome authority."

"Hello!
I wanted to introduce my creator to you!"

"I like her a lot, but she's really stupid,
the poor thing."

"He always looks like he's been
locked in coach for twelve hours.
That's his look."

"There are empty hangers in our wardrobe.
They represent the clothes that would have been completed
by Helmut Lang if he hadn't left."

"Sorry for the spelling mistakes."
"No worries, I work on TV . . ."

"His overwhelming success is proof
that anybody can do it."

"What's your scent?
Tom Ford's pubes?"

"I have nothing to wear. Promise me if I die today,
you'll buy me some other clothes for the coffin."

"Your baby is beautiful.
He's got Nicole Kidman's skin."

"She's committing suicide by bacon."

"No, you're confusing gender and sexuality."
(while eating a potato)

"Does gold rust?"

"I just smoked the joint that puts
Cannes in Saint-Tropez. I can't talk to you."

"It's the daily CVS-ification of everything."

"One night with him is like having
the hiccups in an Ikea metal loft bed."

"She's mostly nice,
but it's her body that's amazing."

"But why didn't you get your license?"
"I stopped at a green light."

"What journalism school did she go to?"
"The Ctrl+C Ctrl+V Institute."

"She super genderized her kids.
So binary . . ."

"It's a dress that makes you feel like
you're in charge of the *whole* open space."

"Her name is Veronica.
It's like Véronique, but in Croatian."

"I can't take any more of these sloppy assistants.
When I started, I used to come to the office wearing Mugler.
You could see the hole from the security tag,
but I was still wearing Mugler."

"My boss showed up at my birthday party
without warning. The shock . . .
It was like Isabelle Huppert showing up in *Twilight*."

"Coffee or champagne?"
"Both."

"It's not about good taste, it's about well-being. Damn,
I sound like a saleswoman for Crocs."

"We filed a patent for the word *mercantile*.
It belongs to us."

"She works at *Madame*."

"She got summa cum laude in snobbery."

"Can you change the color of the series'
subtitles from yellow to white?"
"Of course. And do you want me to reverse the
unemployment trend?"

"My daughter goes to American Apparel
so much that she says,
'I'm going to AmAp.'"

"Doesn't he have a mirror in his place?"

"What's up with this nurse's blouse?"
"Oh, it's nothing. It's an old piece
from the Louis Vuitton collection
with Richard Prince."

"Let's jump cut.
It will look chic."

"You're pretty like a girl."

"She made me swear absolute silence,
but I can tell you."

"I refuse to be bothered
by anything more or less earthly."

"She turned off the music in the editorial office,
yelling, 'Journalism is silence
and a pen!' And then she left for lunch
at Prunier."

"We only offer flowers
to editors. Everything else
gets resold online within the hour."

"She is a real Parisian. She wears Chanel
like it's from a department store and department-store
clothes like they're Chanel."

"Wow. Your ass is as hard as a skull."
"That makes sense. I think with my ass."

"She never says no.
She says,
'My assistant will take your number.'"

"I'm hungry. Do you have any herbal tea?"
"No, just regular tea."
"Just give me hot water then."

"I can't hide anything from my shrink.
She reads the barcode on my head."

"We were young. We drove around in Peugeot 205s
and thought all our problems
could be solved with a nose job."

"Anytime he talks to someone
for more than an hour,
they become a 'friend.'"

"I went to his birthday party.
It was a pool full of pecs."

"She does frivolous but very rigorous
journalism. She'll win the Lily Pulitzer."

"What did you do today?"
"Lunch, beers, dinner."

"We were in Ireland. It was raining so much
that it was raining from the bottom up."

"I work on Avenue Montaigne.
If we made camisoles, we would sell
thousands of them. With rhinestones, of course."

"What is that shade of green?"
"Queen's vomit."

"She's dead. Her obituary on the British *Vogue*
website is covered in Prada ads."

"She doesn't age. I think she lives
at a taxidermy shop."

"You can't stop her, and it's not even
her fault. She's from the planet Guess."

"We only have one life. Let it be fabulous."

"She does all the sample sales.
That's her charity side."

"He did tell me all nothing."

"Just press on her stomach,
and she will tell you horrors for hours.
She's a Parisian woman."

"You remove the bab and
write down the TC of the dead pixels
on the Avid behind the nodal."
(to the trainee who comes out of a business school)

"Frankly, I am going to buy back the wrinkles for her.
The surgeon took the reality off of her face,
the poor thing . . ."

"I bought a table."
"Don't tell me it's a Prouvé."
"Yes, it is, why?"

"Trying to understand my boss is like trying
to recognize a smell in a Sephora."

"When the editor in chief arrives at the office,
we sit down with our hands under our thighs.
It reduces the risk of murder."

"It's the perfect flash to scorch the skin,
thin out the nose, and remove two molars."

"How long is the prison sentence
if you murder a fashion editor in chief?"
"Just a fine, I think."

"I can't write my paper,
nor can I find the right tone to precisely evoke
this moment in life."
"Drink."

"At the end of my dismissal email
it said: 'Sent from my iPad.'"

"It's an article that talks about
the Godardian corpus."

"Deep down, I'm simple, you know."

"Don't take it personally,
she hates the whole world.
Nothing to do with you.
Although less perfume would help."

"Stop thinking she's going to approve of you.
Be yourself."
(trap set for trainee)

"The grandfather was a captain of industry
but the nineteen-year-old grandson is in ninth grade.
It started Caviar Kaspia and it's going to end KFC."

"I'm working in unemployment."

"Last night she dreamed that Chris Christie
was making an H&M collection.
She is in a very bad mood."

"He's Annakareninian."

"Dinner? It was the same as last year
except everyone was a year younger."

"She's dead.
We just need to tell her."

"I'm almost like everyone else."

"I have an idea for a fashion series about purity.
But not the horny purity we've seen too much of.
True, pure purity."

"He's lost a lot of weight, hasn't he?"
"Yes! He broke his jaw."
"On purpose?"

"I love to hate fashion."

"Oh, is it Tuesday?
Tuesday . . . the useless day."

"It was almost as boring
as a supplement about watches."

"How's my hot sand?"

"It's as reliable as the internet connection
in the subway."

"This sun is horrible."

"I'm hungry. Don't you have something to eat
that makes you lose weight?"

"He's a shrewd strategeryist."

"I love deprivation."

"He's handsome, but just for a
pre-fall look-book, not much more."

"Do you know your Aztec sign?"

"I would have loved to be a Leo."

"She thinks the word *really* has a meaning.
With her everything is *really*.
It's *really* nice. It's *really* blue."

"He's coming back from Berlin.
He is slowly recovering from
his night between Friday and Monday."

"Our switchboard operator calls the couriers
luvvy. I want to do a web series on him."

"He's got Warhol paintings like they're plates."

"She has a Bigouden-headdress type of big head."

"Eames is so over."

"When she brainstorms, she forgets to put
the lid on the blender and it splashes everywhere.
It's fantastic."

"Oh shit she's coming towards us
oh no oh shit
oh hello honey how are you?"

"This is the cabinet that was on everyone's lips in Milan."

"His house staff grew old with him.
They have cobwebs in their armpits."

"It's a 'pigeon's blood' ruby; the color is extremely rare."

"I read in the *Times* that teens vape mango and Red Bull.
Do you see yourself managing a kid who vapes Red Bull?"

"He is HRD. He plays Tetris, but with people."

"Who's the stylist?
An old blind friend?"

"I'm so hungry I could eat."

"You don't know Maïmé Arnodin?
She was the one who invented it all.
She invented the trend; she invented black."

"This summer I'm going to Barcelona
and I'm going to be vulgar."

"What about your current affairs?"

"This is Victor."
"Your new boyfriend?"
"Yes. His name is Christophe
but I've had too many Christophes
so I call him Victor."

"Either it's the dumbest idea in the world,
or you'll become a billionaire."
"Or both. The world is full
of stupid billionaires."

"Hello? . . . Hel-lo? Hellohellohello?
Hello? Hello? Hello?
Yes, I can hear you very well."

"These are heels designed to be seen
the other way around. Legs in the air."

"She's semi-rich.
Acné is her Zara."

"You really are an easy guy."
"Not more than the others."

"They should do a Metro pass
for the fashion shows.
It would save me from having
my mailbox overflowing with invitations."

"Well, I wouldn't have retouched the jaw like that."
(flipping through a magazine)

"I just saw such a sublime yellow flower."
"You, who doesn't like yellow."
"I know. But it inspired me."

"I was on the Google Beach in Cannes."

"He just put his initials
on his intercom. He thinks he's famous."

"You are cut like a V;
I am cut like an O."

"He lives in France; success is not his thing."

"With him time passes as if you were untangling
the wires on your headphones for hours and hours."

"I don't do married guys.
Well, not anymore."

"He's a little milky, but he's very handsome."

"He hasn't read anything, but he's twenty
so he's still the one who's right."

"She goes in an evening dress to the bakery.
Well, she doesn't go to the bakery,
but you know what I mean."

"She only says great bullshit.
When she talks, it's raining honey."

"I just had my energies redistributed.
It feels great; I'm back on track."

"It's smart fashion, but who cares?"

"He is editor in chief of *Mall Magazine* in Dubai.
I don't know if you can imagine the power of the guy."

"The dress code for dinner is Pantone 1935.
And beware: solid Pantone. Plain."
"Meaning?"
"Dark fuchsia."

"Tonight I'm going out and having problems
with vodka and pretty girls."

"This is our novelty:
suitcases without wheels."

"No, it's not quite white. It's steamy."

"Do we believe in blue laces?"

"I don't have time to clean;
it's too earthly."

"No need to try to go to art galleries
this weekend; they're all going to be
showrooms for black clothing."

"Since when has *adorable* become an insult?"

"Hello."
"Hello, we would like a salad and four place settings."
"A salad for four?"
"Yes, thank you!"

"He's a little too tattooed.
When he's naked it's like Harlequin."

"My thirteen-year-old daughter just got her ass."

"I fall in love every two minutes."

"He's awesome. So far in the stratosphere . . ."

"The profile of the intern we are looking for
is Ivy league–Givenchy Couture."

"My daughter respects nothing,
except new clothes."

"He confuses swallowing as many consonants as possible
with having fun."

"In English this flower is called baby's breath."

"He has a French beauty."

"When you think about it,
you know it's better not to think about it."

"He is beautiful. But an unfair kind of beautiful."

"I'm in a week where I'm not doing
too much shopping. It almost disgusts me.
And next week I'll do it night and day."

"Don't bring a present;
your presence is already a gift.
At least, no books."

"It's too hard, I can't take it anymore,
I really can't find sunglasses."

"She is worse than a Parisian.
I don't know if you can imagine."

"They found a guy in a suitcase two years ago.
Last night they reconstructed
the crime in front of my place."

"What's his name already?
This dictator called Kim?"

"We sexted a lot when I was depressed.
It distracted me.
It helped me."

"At the gym, her flask is a bottle
of champagne she fills with water."

"What was that color?"
"Rotten apricot."

"You know the gap between Instagram
and reality? Well, he lives in that ditch."

"If his muscles could talk he might have been smart."

"You know, your snobbery will always
be someone else's trivia."

"She's cute but too much.
She's got pink blood in her veins
and candy bones."

"I don't do drugs."
"You took mushrooms and smoked last weekend."
"That's not drugs."

"It was a fairly quiet dinner. It got out of hand
when we started to figure out which character
from *In Search of Lost Time* Kim K is."

"He's stupid like lukewarm sparkling water."

"She thinks she's over the Internet."

"How was your night?"
"I lost my dignity."
"Define *lost*."

"After the Fashion Special, the Hair Special,
and the Perfume Special,
the next issue will be an Advertisers Special;
it's easier."

"I'm trying to start a company.
We're going to screw it up,
but it's super exciting."

"No, you do the selfie,
your arm is longer."

"She ditched him by explaining to him
that she didn't have the time."

"I originally wanted to work in the fashion industry,
not the compromise industry."

"I don't know him, but I hate him."

"It's black."
"No, it's blackbird."

"It's a perfume symbolizing surrendering to love.
Blackcurrant buds, sandalwood, vanilla."

"His iPhone is one of his organs."

"It was really an urge to reinvent black."
(speaking about a white shirt)

"Is it too much?"
"You know, you've already crossed the border of too much—
you've invaded the country,
overthrown the government,
and killed the people."

"She's either on a diet or eating
or eating talking about dieting
or dieting talking about eating."

"I have a bad idea
that I need to talk to you about."

"It's a raindrop-scented candle."

"They had equal qualifications.
So I hired the one with the
best Twitter account."

"It's weird to always want to go
to the same restaurant, to the same club,
to always want to relive the same evening,
the same weekend."

"She Photoshops her two-month-old baby."

"There are so many gays in my neighborhood
that my Grindr doesn't go
more than sixty feet away."

"She eats men and spits out diamonds."

"Does he have friends?"
"Friendship isn't his problem."

"Is that a radiator or a sculpture?"
"A sculpture."
"Ah, sorry. It's pretty anyway."

"He's agoraphobic right now,
so he led the photo shoot through Skype."

"I have a very human documentary project
on the economic crisis in the North."
"The north of Paris?"

"It was very stupid; it made me think of you."

"She loves bad news;
she's always the first to announce
a death on Twitter."

"The entire editorial team hates her.
When she talks we go into airplane mode."

"She dumped him by mutual agreement."

"He's unemployed.
Well, screenwriter."

"She's a hearty eater.
She eats as much as you don't."

"It smells like oil, doesn't it?
Is anyone here wearing something from
the H&M Alexander Wang collection?"

"No, you don't say 'Saint Laurent Paris'!
It's like saying 'Prada Milano'
or 'Chanel 31 rue Cambon.'"

"My new apartment is awfully big.
There is an echo when I speak.
I have to make phone calls from the balcony.
And I'm cold."

"I'm so tired I can't sleep anymore."

"He's a real tough guy.
You can't see his tattoos
because he's tattooed on the inside."

"There were a million people
on his birthday. There was Kate Moss
and a hashtag."

"You're beautiful tonight."
"Yes."

"How do you wash it?"
"You don't wash it. You put it on once,
everyone sees you with it, and you throw it away."

"I loved her.
She was Yves and Sagan's dealer."

"Do you think he's a liar?"
"No. He's not smart enough to invent."

"You don't say *meh*; you say *fantastic editorial crush*.
You don't say *routine*;
you say *extremely well-oiled choreography*."

"I would bang him
but he would have to shut up."

"When it comes to makeup,
she goes Halloween all year round."

"There was a fire and she shouted, 'Save the furs!'
But I decided to save the mood board."

"With clothes like that
she doesn't need enemies."

"Shrinks say that handbags are vaginas."
"Oh dear, the museum security guys
open bags all day . . ."

"For the theme of the collection,
we hesitated between Russian Porcelain and Fluorescent Techno."
"So what did you do?"
"Leopard Panther."

"You're at the crucial moment when you decide
to either grow old or rejuvenate. Either way
people will say you've become awful."

"Don't say *ugly*; say *artisanal*.
Don't say *corny*; say *heritage*."

"He has a diet that consists of reading French novels
and eating chicken. It works."

"What's the matter? Looks like you've seen
death or a tube of mayonnaise."

"Don't take a picture of me here;
I'm fake-gramming that I'm by a pool."

"He died with tremendous grace."

"You look beautiful; you should take a selfie."

"If it only rained on idiots,
he would wear Burberry all year round."

"Let's say she designs clothes
for people who don't need
to make love."

"I made a big decision this weekend in Amsterdam."
"You're crazy, you should never decide anything
in Amsterdam."

"Can I have a day,
just a day, a small day,
without pain?"
(tasting a warm Coke Zero)

"Him? On a misunderstanding
at two in the morning I wouldn't say no."

"Who's the editor in chief?"
"Choupette."

"Her art collection is a
Who's Who of mistakes."

"She just got married for the fourth time.
I've been to more of her weddings
than her birthday parties."

"She's smart, in quotes."

"They missed their plane; we had to pay for a jet.
They arrived dead drunk
and not a thank-you, not a tweet."

"I was hungry;
I swallowed my chewing gum."

"If the publicist has a big head,
that means the creator has a big head.
It's a big-head pyramid."

"At Chanel, it's chic. They didn't write
'Standing' on my invitation but 'Row Z.'"

"I worked in consulting and I was taken for a psycho.
Now I'm in fashion and I'm normal."

"It was awesome.
It will be ugly when worn
but it is a real innovation!"

"We don't say *mini*.
We'd rather say *maxi short*."

"Kissing the designer at the end of the fashion show
is like kissing the metal bar of the Metro.
That's why Anna kisses them before the show."

"At Gaultier I caught my assistant
googling Catherine Deneuve.
He didn't know who she was."

"She wants me to be *serious* . . .
I told her there are enough people
in the world like that."

"The talent to be talked about is
as important as talent itself."

"Don't walk with your legs crossed.
Walk modern."

"It's not beige.
It's natural white."

"She's adorable."
"Yes, that's her job."

"The dresses were long; that was indecent."

"Can you take a selfie of me?"

"There were no written invitations.
Those who thought they were invited presented themselves."

"I have to go feed my cat before I go to Lanvin."

"You should stop noting everything,
Shazaming, filming everything,
and start enjoying it a bit."

"Anna isn't here today.
She's at George Clooney's wedding."

"Oh look, resting pickpockets.
Tourists must be having lunch."

"They are in sneakers. They disgust me.
They don't make any effort with their feet."

"I had decided to drink tea,
but give me some vodka."

"Did you like it?"
"I loved it."
"What would you wear?"
"Nothing, I didn't like the clothes
but the energy."

"I don't understand my bag."

"What does she do for a living?"
"She creates clicks."

"Dumbass."
"Who?"
"This day."

"She's perfect twenty-eight hours a day.
Horrible."

"Better to do it too much than to regret
not doing it at all."

"I know her well. She adores me.
I'll lend you her plane."

"The genius idea is to have removed
one of the handles from the bag to create
this so-modern imbalance."

"I need the ocean and a burger."

"He only photographed people
who have since died . . . We call him
Père Lachaise."

"Until I thank the audience
at the end of a Dior show
my parents will never understand what I do in life."

"Who cares about perfection?
We want intensity."

"There aren't enough emojis
for my emotions. I want a lot more."

"She has a private mansion for hosting,
an apartment for clothes,
and an apartment for sleeping."

"You know that left brain, right brain thing? Well,
she's got a shoe brain and a bag brain."

"It's a burger but it's not a burger.
It's a reinvented burger, without bread;
it's a woman's burger."
(seriously)

"The inspiration is a girl riding a bicycle on a volcano."

"She's a good client. She buys a lot.
We call her the Vacuum Cleaner."

"Is she nice nice or obnoxious nice?
Because I know hateful people
who are nice and vice versa."

"One day her wardrobe will collapse
and suffocate her. A happy death."

"She's quick to understand nothing."

"He is in the top five of the
most difficult creators to give a gift to.
Karl, with Choupette, it was easy."

"Your nail polish is sublime."
"Yes, it's like a black red, except it's green."

"Stop thinking logical.
Think fashion."

"Are those skinny jeans or did you get fat?"

"Be careful! Don't kiss!
You both have embroidered tops, they'll get caught!
It'll take two hours to separate you."

"Life is difficult; we don't do what we want."
"Speak for yourself."

"I don't know how you do it. If I heard myself
I would hate myself."

"Don't give him an interview.
He has the new triple HD camera
that makes the skin purple,
with every pore a crater."

"These are not industrial prices but emotional prices.
They are based on the value they will have
in the head of the customer."

"Be polite when you call. Use your Chanel voice."

"It's horrible how everything is
becoming normal."

"Her profession is Selfie."

"She's cold and considerate.
She's not a woman, she's an algorithm."

"Congratulating a designer for music
is like telling a novelist whose book you just read
that his hair looks good."

"Don't film me, I'm too fat,
with me your card will say Memory Full right away."

"Your sweater is nice."
"I know. Celine."

"She's a great person and I don't want to ruin her.
So I left her."

"Because of the Air France strike,
the Paris-Milan EasyJet this morning
was a moment of humility.
You didn't hear a single Hermès bracelet tinkle."

"You look OK but you don't put yourself out there.
Still, it's better than all those ugly people
who overextend themselves."

"Her wonder capacity is at zero.
Keep it short."

"Red meat is like Prada:
If you really want it, just go for it."

"Money makes her annoying.
She'd almost be better off poor."

"No one is chic. Everybody *moche*."

"The way she dresses every day,
I wonder how she gets dressed
when she really goes to a wedding."

"This is python that we rubbed off
to give it a python effect."
"You de-pythoned to re-python?"
"Yes."

"Jay-Z came onstage and started to scream
Tom Ford Tom Ford Tom Ford
for five minutes."

"Love your look. It's . . . colorful . . ."
"Thank you. There is too much negativity
in the world, so I wanted to spread some joy."

"Oh yes, let's have a great lunch!
Email me at the end of next month!"

"He has the body to open doors
at Abercrombie."

"I slept with him last night."
"Ah, me too, the day before yesterday; he's cool."

"I'm a Lebanese woman stuck
in a male French body."

"I love your Mercedes tattoo."
"No, it's the peace symbol."
"Oh! There are so many logos now . . ."

"I have a lot of books at home.
All the sneaker literature."

"I have my bikes stolen so much in Paris
that now I buy them in pairs."

"No more than three colors on an outfit.
Right now you look like a plastic rainbow."

"On the model, it's a mermaid dress.
On the client it will be a whale dress."

"He's a model and an environmental engineer."
"You mean he's a beautiful gardener?"

"This town doesn't understand you.
In Berlin you would become a star.
You would become a rumor."

"Did you sleep with him?"
"No idea."

"I'm hungry, I could eat a model."

"No, you don't Instagram yourself in the helicopter.
It's too hick.
You can take a selfie in the Rolls.
But only if it's vintage."

"She dresses like a swinger."

"My biggest fear is waking up
after a night out without
remembering what I did.
And I know that fear very well."

"Love the real void of August compared to
the fake full of September."

"I'm going to bed, I have to go
to *Vogue* early in the morning."

"Come on, grab your iPad,
we're going to the beach."

"He called his dog Mister.
He addresses it as *vous*.
It's a very well-mannered dog."

"She's at that point of vacation
where a game of Uno is too intense."

"He's a waiter in New York. He thinks rosé
is red wine mixed with white wine."

"I slept with him. He makes love
like popcorn in the microwave."

"Do you want grapes?"
"No, I'd rather not, they're fatty."

"What's the secret to your longevity?"
"The whims."

"All the paintings I own are creepy.
For me art must be sinister.
A cute painting is like a
smiling model."

"I believe you–ish."

"At forty you erase everything and start over."
(Biotherm slogan)

"I have a flight tomorrow to go to Milan
to try on the dress. What a pain . . ."

"I have just returned from Brittany. It was so sunny.
The weather is nice, like when we were kids."

"She is a Mona Lisa press agent.
No one will ever know
what's behind that smile."

"It's the last of my thirty-fifth birthdays,
next year will be my first thirty-ninth."

"She's as sweet as a free Chanel suit."

"They were dancing imitating the movement of
'the arm taking a selfie.'
It was sublime."

"What happened to him?
Have there been any sales at Lindt?"

"In Paris they all are graphic designers,
in Berlin they are DJs, and
in the rest of the world
they are visual merchandisers."

"Love it. It's like a printed Tumblr."
(flipping through a photo book)

"She peeled his heart.
I can tell you he's cooked."

"Does this brand still exist?"
"Yes, but now it's done by interns."

"The collections that everyone likes
are bad collections."

"Sorry, she's not doing any more interviews right now,
she's closed for renovations."

"It's not a lie;
it's a contextual truth."

"She made her fortune in fair trade."

"He has German legs
and a Portuguese heart:
in shape and sentimental."

"I emptied my closet to throw it all away
but put it all back in.
It was too beautiful."

"The guy hits on you with a deep voice
and then drinks his vodka with a straw."

"It must be crazy sleeping with someone
who has such perfect proportions."
"You're becoming a surveyor."

"No thanks. It's an even year, no carbs."

"Are you OK?
Your gaze is lost in regrets . . ."

"Your forties are when you still don't understand anything
but you know things."

"I made high pockets because
I wanted to revolutionize the posture of
the arms on the body."

"I'm not a snob."
(at the Flore terrace)

"Do you think the guy who invented
the sound of the kiss receives royalties
every time?"

"Yesterday evening it was
red heart flamenco, red heart flamenco,
but this morning
it's gun, skull, gun."

"I am Parisian. I have the Seine
running through my veins."

"I try not to look at Instagram
on the weekends.
I need limits."

"I don't read *People*, I live *People*."

"It's a thousand-hour embroidery dress
made to be worn for two hours and ripped off."

"She is impervious to guilt.
Try positive manipulation instead."

"I ate as if I had no beach in ten days."

"Are you OK?"
"Yes. I'm a bit dead
but it's a beautiful death."

"Did you Shazam during Chanel?"
"No, I didn't have time, I was going crazy
over the dresses."

"She's a drama queen, she turns
commas into exclamation marks."

"The thing is, I'm pretty beautiful
in black-and-white from afar,
but real life is colorful and close."

"How did you get your tattoo done?
With a fork?"

"Her boyfriend is the Mount Vesuvius of money.
A permanent eruption of molten cash."

"Have you seen her rings?
I think she has two bodyguards
just for her little finger."

"The helicopter isn't that expensive, either."

"Luxury ready-to-wear
is for the one percent.
Couture is for the 0.000001 percent."

"The only affordable things
are the coats at $15,000.
You can forget the rest."

"I feel like I've been spoiled
in my life, but this . . ."
(in Hermès from head to toe,
describing their weekend)

"Oh my God, what happened to you?"
"Oh, nothing, that's a poppers burn."

"When will you give birth?"
"August."
"Well done! You won't miss the fashion shows."

"He's handsome, but he's resting
on his genetic laurels."

"I loved him when he was talented."

"She's sick?"
"No, it's the makeup."

"We have to have a meeting
to prepare for the meeting."

"Do we buy a Kindle for the boat?"
"Darling, you don't read enough
for a Kindle."

"There was a cash thunderstorm
and she was struck full blast."

"She's turning her Giacometti into a lamp."
"Does she have the right?"
"She's doing it."

"People want filthy bling.
That's what hits the mark."

"She is a hard drive of nastiness.
When she dies, all those humiliating
methods will disappear with her . . ."

"She smokes and she sleeps. That's all."

"How was it?"
"Minimalist and quick."
"Nothing?"
"The good kind of nothing."

"He has such a big head . . .
He pees perfume."

"I'm on the edge of having the cheeseburger . . ."

"My job is my hobby."
"And vice versa."

"One thing's for sure: Ugly has a future."

"She's only talking about herself
and fictional characters."

"We'll try to have lunch around 5 PM."

"I am going around in circles.
I should be connected to a generator;
I would light up all of Paris."

"Even his anger is elegant."

"We have a family dinner with muses
and *Vogue*'s editors in chief."

"What is it?"
"Oh, nothing, it's Valentino from a hundred seasons ago."

"My hookup from yesterday didn't speak
English, French, or Italian.
He spoke body language."

"Don't say *crazy*, say *amazing*.
Don't say *dead drunk*, say *incandescent*."

"It's a perfume inspired by
the smell of wet stones."

"I had 255 likes on the photo in twenty-five minutes!"
"You realize it's one second for Beyoncé?"

"What is your hidden talent?"
"Humility."

"My ex is narcissistic and obsessed with me."
"Just like you."

"I've never met someone
so unfair, and I work in fashion."

"Have you eaten?"
"Yes, Coke Zero."

"We don't have a budget,
but we'll pay you in shoes, OK?"

"The secret is to always tell him no
but in a positive way."

"I'm a little ashamed, but I don't like
New York. It doesn't galvanize me . . .
I like Athens a hundred times more."

"We do fashion, not subtlety."

"I come from the Paris region."
"Where?"
"Nice."

"I love my hairdresser.
He doesn't have a big head."

"Anyone can be gorgeous,
no matter the foundation they start with."

"Oh no, I didn't see that Balenciaga show.
I was in custody."

"When he falls in love,
he'll think he's sick."

"I hope that your tattoo hurt you less
than it hurts my eyes."

"She's very pretentious.
She dresses in Jean Prouvé."

"At my office, they all have
the same Celine Trapeze bag
that they think is pale eggshell
but really is butter."

"He ate my heart while saying yuck."

"Don't, *don't* take a picture of me.
I'm not photogenic from December to April."

"She doesn't love anyone. Not even herself."

"We had a dinner without a photographer.
It was amazing!"

"I have a great new fishmonger on my street."

"I work in the celebrity acquisition
department of a communications firm."

"She lives alone, with her hair and jewelry."

"I hate my hands.
I want to cut them off."

"I love to cry."

"They have situational beauty.
Without the uniform, it's not as good."

"The engagement rate with my body was
a little too high last night."

"Visually, it's gonna hurt."

"She had a single-product business model
and didn't survive the leggings crisis."

"She has more Louboutin shoes than neurons.
"Yes, and she doesn't have that many Louboutins."

"What day is Thursday?"

"My eyes are down the back of my neck,
and my mouth is above my ear.
A casual Sunday."

"My assistant doesn't know who I am."

"You should never ask me a mean question
because my answer will be worse."

"I am expected to give her a gift
to thank her, but I hesitate
between a bouquet and a stuffed hyena."

"We have such a long waiting list for interns
that they are forty-five when they start
working with us."

"She bought herself a Chloé coat
that's so beautiful she wears it all the time.
She does her meetings in this coat."

"You want a coffee?"
"Never. I drink cappuccino
but only in Japan."

"It's not white. It's plaster."

"Hello? Yes, hello, Karl.
Yes, very good, and you?"

"My life is a GIF."

"I love him. He could throw up in my mouth."

"Did they stretch you out with Photoshop
in the photo taken in Marrakech?"
"No way!"
"For me, they always slim under my underthigh."

"I hate this."
"But you loved it this morning!"
"Yes. This morning. I'm not
the same person anymore!"

"She's embarrassing—
like turquoise at a wedding."

"It's not about looking clean,
it's about acting clean."

"No. I don't sign autographs.
I'm the hairstylist for the stars,
but I'm not the star."

"Are you telling me yes or no?"
"Certainly! One of the two."

"We copied it from a Belgium designer,
but who cares?
It's not who did it first that matters,
but who pushed it the strongest in the stores."

"I'm starting a new treatment that uses waves.
The guy does not touch your skin,
but your face looks as if
you had been embalmed at twenty-three."

"Oh boy, I'm having lunch with Kristen Stewart.
I'm going to have to speak English."

"Don't say *weird*, say *hybrid*.
Don't say *heavy*, say *telluric*.
And never say *ugly*."

"This is our new Nude Air zero-matter
serum that has a bare-skin effect."

"You put too much on."
"Of what?"
"Of everything."

"She is a very good Russian client—
father in the KGB, extremely wealthy,
pure product of kleptocracy.
Or is she Swiss? I don't remember."

"What is that color?"
"Soja."

"Did you give birth? Are you happy?
See, it was worth missing
a season of fashion shows, right?"

"I love this moment before the fashion show—
during the tenth sleepless night—
when you feel complete."

"You have to come to Taiwan!"
"I will! I will!"
(both glued to their respective phones)

"The fashion show was packed.
I think I stepped on the equivalent
of 300,000 dollars' worth of Saint Laurent shoes."

"Do you know each other?"
"No, we've never met but we love each other."

"I'm sick."
"Me too, but I got dead drunk
at the Louis Vuitton party yesterday.
It killed the germs."

"What is this material? It makes my eyes itch."

"I try to relax a bit with work.
For example, now I avoid emails
after midnight."

"I love your embroidered sweater,
but how do you wash it?"
"Oh, you just don't wash it.
You don't wash fashion anymore!"

"How was the fashion show?"
"Meh. Like Christmas Eve with vegetarians."

"It was the fashion show that made me
reconcile with everything."
"Ah, I wasn't there."
"That's why you're still angry."

"It's a non-foaming shampoo.
We call it no-poo."

"She has gotten sidelined.
She reads the dates and names of the saints
in her Hermès diary and that's it."

"She lives in one of those towns
that are fun for two or three days in August."

"I was at this party last night
where there were maybe three non-mutants."

"What do you prefer?
To have no heart or no butt?"

"I don't know his name,
but he has a face that should be called *beige*."

"Basically, they offered me a permanent contract
but not paid."

"What is your project with your hair?"

"This is a dress I love.
I even wore it twice."

"Looks like my sex life."
(looking at the traffic on Place de l'Étoile)

"What is it?"
"An unscented candle."

"I won't be at the fashion shows.
I have a fling in Austria."

"That's ugly."
"Yes, but it's cleverly ugly."

"I had an argument with everyone today."
"With everyone?"
"Yes, in my head."

"You look happy."
"Yes, that's the amazing new moisturizer."

"I care just as much as a fish would
about a Versace dress."

"If they are advertisers,
you remove the question marks.
If they're big advertisers,
you add exclamation points."

"Was the vacation good? Were there lots of penises?"

"I went to a fashion show once.
It's crazy to put so much money
into doing such a boring thing."

"Is he handsome?"
"He has 20,000 Instagram followers
with twenty photos."
"Oh, OK, he's handsome."

"I'm a pleasure activist."

"He's really sexual.
Well, right now he ate a little too much turkey,
but he's really sexual."

"And you, what do you do to disconnect?"
(without listening to the answer)

"I am not a physiognomist.
I'm much more savvy in fashion.
I recognize the dresses but not the faces."

"He has a mental illness that means
he can't stand imperfection."
"Oh yes, I have that too!"

"She lectured me about 'real life,'
while she has had her head
in the clouds for years."

"My hairstyle is good, but as soon as I land
in Lebanon it's going to be horrible.
Beirut is the worst thing that can happen to hair."

"These are my favorite shoes.
I can't walk in them,
but that's the only flaw."

"The guy I thought was cute just twerked."

"She's marquise lame."

"Affordable is like wearable, it's useless."

"What's that look? Are you taking a walk
around the hospital?"

"Was it a good party on Saturday?"
"My white shoes are now black."

"She loves hiking, but only in sandals."

"I had to move away from my street."
"Poor thing."
"Yes, too many bakeries were opening.
It was horrible."

"Stop your value judgments."
"I work in fashion; I make a value judgment every minute.
It's my talent. I'm paid for it."

"For Christmas, I will offer hieroglyphics lessons
to my boyfriend."

"He canceled all of his interviews
because of a testicular torsion.
Needless to say, I didn't tell you anything."

SEASON 2015

"Happy New Year!"
"You too.
Have a nice dip in an empty swimming pool."

"I dreamed that you were getting crushed
by a giant J'adore Dior poster."

"I'm old enough to write my memoirs
but too old to be able
to remember anything."

"Ah . . . if his fingers could talk."

"I have a great new GP,
I got the number from my friends at Chanel."

"Thanks, but I can't eat
with the sleeves of this jacket I have on."

"You're in Paris. Not in your dreams."

"I'm not a diva. We live an ordinary life."

"You have dandruff."
"No, that's the print of my shirt."

"He has a privacy switch. In two minutes
you think he's your confidante."

"I want to feel like the one percent."

"No, it's Julyen with a *y*."

"I need to do a thousand-piece jigsaw puzzle."

"He was Daft Punk's hairdresser
before they put the helmets on."

"Have you checked your emails?"
"I don't have an email address."

"You look so beautiful! What is your diet?"
"Depression."
"Oh great!"

"There is no color in my home's interior
because people are the color of the room."

"I saw Catherine Deneuve smoking a cigarette
in the restaurant so I lit mine,
but then they came and asked me to put it out."

"What did you do this weekend?"
"I don't remember."

"You look beautiful!"
"Stop it, it's Zara."

"You were very beautiful yesterday!"
"Ah? Not today?"

"As an aperitif, we will enjoy
ibuprofen tarts."

"You turned down the job?"
"Yes, it was on the G line of the subway."

"I heard 300 rumors about Dior.
At the end of the day, I wanted to scream at them,
But which Dior are you talking about?"

"The inspiration is the '60s
but not the literal '60s—
more like the '60s
if they hadn't been the '60s."

"You know there are going to be
Balmain × H&M people in our lives next week?
I hope you've prepared yourself psychologically."

"So who's your target tonight?"
"Everyone."

"Awful Halloween party.
The ones that weren't in disguise looked like
the disguised ones."

"We brainstormed all night about the buttons."

"Have a good weekend?"
"I didn't budge.
I became the armrest of the sofa."

"That's pretty, what is it?"
"The T-shirt? Gap."
"I envy you. You're lucky to be able to wear
something other than Celine.
I can't."

"Anna Wintour wrote about the subway in her editorial.
The story was from 1981."

"It's nice to meet you.
You're less ugly than in the picture."

"What's her news?"
"Gastric banding surgery."

"She goes out a lot.
She dresses in tablecloths from Maxim's."

"She has a guest castle."

"You know, for her, luxury is a night
where no one takes a picture of her."

"Want a cookie?"
"No, I'm in Versace."

"How do we credit you?
Maquilleur or makeup artist?"
"I prefer that you write: Skin.
Just that."

"How was the party?"
"There were 800 iPhones on two It girls."

"She's rich. She's got a rich laugh."

"A guy leaving when he wakes up—the dream."

"We don't say *knot*, it's negative.
We prefer to say *twin wings of freedom*.
It's more positive."

"She has a night body.
In the daytime, she's not that great,
but after midnight she's sublime."

"Don't say *salesperson*, say *client partner*."

"I love going to the movies.
It's a nice change from watching a TV series.
You're done in two hours!"

"She was beautiful at thirty, gorgeous at forty,
and since then, the more wrinkles she has,
the chicer she gets."

"I live in the bubble of a bubble of a bubble."

"I am an outdoor designer."
"Garden gardener?"
"Yes, that's it."

"He is not bad but he has a bit too many ideas."

"The teachers are so mean at her fashion school.
You wonder if it's not the nastiness they teach them."

"I dreamed about Gucci."

"You think I'm a designer but I'm a storyteller."

"Our editor in chief always wears the same thing.
We don't know if it's a shirt or a fossil anymore."

"Hello, honey, what's your first name again?"

"Are you drawing silhouettes?"
"No. I'm writing a word every now and then
on a Post-it for the studio."

"She dresses in Dior from Zara."

"I know you, don't I?"
"No, I don't think so.
I was in a viral video two years ago.
Maybe that's it?"

"I feel empty."
"I'm not surprised."

"So how was it?
Tell me as many details as possible.
I wasn't there
but I have to write an article."

"How do you make your white so white?"
"I wash it in Ardèche:
There is less limestone
and it comes out brilliant."

"My assistant lost the fantastic bag
you gave me. Do you have any left?
I love it so much."

"I would like to have a love affair
with an intern from Vetements,
something pure."

"She was born outside Paris.
She was raised by wolves."

"You can ask her questions tomorrow,
but come dressed in black so you don't disturb
the creative process."

"I'm bored. It's not bad but I'm bored.
I'm beautifully bored."

"How was your weekend in Madrid?
What did you do?"
"Very good. I read the phone book with my ass."

"He's very well surrounded,
but his entourage's entourage sucks."

"She dresses any old way!"
"It's her job."

"She has the same butt as Kim K
but without the millions of followers.
Totally useless."

"Do you prefer shrimp or beef?"
"Depends, are you talking about food or guys?"

"Self-mockery is what's most important.
Everyone is so serious.
They're serious even in bed."

"Language isn't his thing."

"Is she a muse or an ambassador?"
"Her official status is Faithful to the House."

"I love the energy of your dress."

"She's as sad as a day without a Chanel logo."

"Hello? Yes, I did receive the dress as a gift.
Thank you very much, but you forgot
to remove the security tag from the store."

"Anna requires meetings with no more than two people
and that are no longer than ten minutes."

"I'm touching her! I'm touching her!
I'M TOUCHING HER!"
(touching Rihanna)

"I forgot to send you flowers but you get the idea."

"The marketing department just took over.
They're going to rename the brand Panic."

"Sorry, but who is the guy
I just introduced you to?"

"It was beautiful and I lost my mind.
I left with the whole store in my shopping bags.
But without their lighting it was lousy,
so I returned it all."

"I love circles. My style is full of circles.
I wish seeing a circle would make people think of me."

"He's as soft as a 69 with a mink."

"I got an invitation that says,
'first row access.' Am I first row?"
"No, but you have the right to film the first row."

"I don't know why they invite her.
She doesn't even get 2,000 likes per photo."

"I dreamed I was eating."

"What are you wearing?"
"It's a silk from 1910."
"How do you wash it?"
"You don't wash it, you aerate it."

"She goes to all the fashion dinners with caviar.
When she throws up, it's black."

"Can we do the post-fashion show interview
with the designer?"
"Ah, it would be a pleasure but he's gone."

"He was almost normal after rehab,
and we believed it,
but then Satan came back."

"How was the music at the fashion show?"
"Like a rich six-year-old's birthday party."

"I shouldn't have slept
with my furniture history teacher."

"She's important.
She has an encrypted Samsung."

"Everything became too fancy.
I'm hungry for vulgarity."

"The inspiration is a trash bag, but elegant."

"She erased the facelift she had done in Korea.
Customs officials didn't recognize her on her passport."

"I drank a Red Bull champagne with Philipp Plein.
It was horrible. It was awesome.
It was horrible."

"Do you have children?"
"Yes, I think one or two."

"I haven't drunk water for a very long time."

"This is the contradiction between the past and the present."
(explaining a diamond print)

"*Vogue*, to me, is a family album."

"The inspiration is the last 600 years."

"He's an artist.
I quite like his work
but his Instagram is better."

"Don't make me laugh.
It causes wrinkles."

"Kanye called wanting to come to the fashion show with Kim.
We said no, not Kim. She's not our image.
So he came over and left her in the car."

"I want to swallow beauty."

"Don't you want champagne? I want champagne."
"Now, on a Monday?"
"No, it's Friday! Are you sure it's Monday?"

"Don't say *bimbo*, say *free*."

"She is super charming.
Looks like a brand publicist
who isn't an advertiser."

"It's superblime."

"I don't know what you're doing here.
I don't give interviews anymore."

"The inspiration is banana,
things that peel off the body."

"What did you do this summer?"
"Camping. Something that was very deconnective."

"With this courtesy rule that forbids me
to sleep with your exes,
there's no one left for me in this town."

"Don't say *blogger*, say *content creator*."

"I loved it thirty seconds ago
but I don't like it anymore."

"She's great.
It's too bad I don't like what she does."

"During the fashion shows, everything accelerates.
Each day lasts an hour.
What time is it? Tuesday."

"She was the worst head seamstress ever.
If I jumped because of a pin, she said,
'I'll give you a reason to scream,'
and she'd poke me."

"Restaurants are empty."
"I know, everyone's in New York."

"She's so rich she doesn't blush anymore."

"You're OK for the interview,
but in five seasons when he's ready.
It's humility, not pretension, you know."

"I was on the street this morning around 8 AM
and it was packed!
People actually get up very early.
Shocking!"

"Your hair is horrible."
"Yes, I know."
"No, but like really horrible."

"She's a very good friend of mine."
"What's her last name?"
"I don't know."

"What is that color?"
"Damp purple."

"Don't say *pink*, say *light grenadine*."

"I want a Hermès umbrella."
"I *need* a Hermès umbrella."

"That was forty years ago, in 1997."
"1997 wasn't forty years ago."
"Of course it was."

"I'm at work."
"But there's not much to do in August, right?"
"I write myself emails to pretend I'm working."

"Don't look at me.
I've had a long conversation with potatoes this summer."

"I love him.
But it's true that I have an incredible boredom tolerance."

"Where is the Cannes Film Festival this year?"

"She lost all notion about the reality
of the epidermis."

"How was the party?"
"It started when you arrived."

"If you go to Vienna, I know
a great Airbnb apartment that's
very close to Michael Haneke's place."

"She is in a very good mood when she wakes up.
She's a freak."

"I'm tanned like
a *Big Brother* finalist."

"Have you heard? It's awesome!"
"What?"
"You don't know? Oh no, I won't be the one to tell you."
"But what?"
"Nothing."

"The only Italian word Liz Taylor knew
was *Bulgari*."

"I love this model.
Looks like she's going to talk."

"But why didn't you tell me?"
"I'm telling you now."

"I would like to take a nap and wake up
two weeks ago."

"Have you booked the beach for tomorrow?"
"We're on the waiting list."

"Luckily the vacation ends soon,
then I'll be able to rest."

"What did you *not* do today?"

"I hate sand."

"It's dark black."

"How's your vacation?
Not too generic?"

"We played which model are you?
You should have seen how stressful it was."

"Let go. It doesn't make much of a difference for you.
Have fun with your demons."

"Is that fog or pollution?"
"No idea."

"Can you have sex without dating?"
"Yes, it's called vacation."

"I feel as useless as a sign saying
'Watch Out for Pickpockets' in a backroom."

"We're on a boat.
We don't have access to social media,
but the moon is sublime. It almost consoles me."

"You smell good. You smell like the sun."

"You have an aggressiveness
toward happiness that appeals to me."

"You look exhausted."
"Yes, I'm on vacation."

"Hello, could you give me the password
for the beach Wi-Fi, please?"

"It was a packed party. There were no more glasses,
so I had to drink from a vase."

"I thought you were at the movies?"
"Yes, I was, but my phone wasn't getting any signal
so I came back home."

"He's a noninvasive dermatologist."

"It's a purse that says fuck the planet."

"In her report, the intern talks about us
as if we were a time machine."

"We were supposed to talk about work,
but he only talked about gossip.
In fact, he gossips about himself.
He's a self-tattletale."

"She is important in fashion.
It's *Clothegentsia*."

"She loves designer furniture.
She only rests her ass
on famous chairs."

"I'm going on vacation to the south of vulgarity."

"This cream contains golden root extract and
provides intense and continuous
moisture for thirty hours."

"Her villa is fine,
but she heats her pool too much."

"I washed my Prada T-shirt at ninety degrees.
It became a Miu Miu T-shirt."

"Frankly, going to the gym so much
only to dress like that,
well, you might as well not do anything."

"If Hedi Slimane has never done it, we look stupid,
and if he did it, it's too late."

"How high are your heels?"
"It's not about inches, it's a lifestyle."

"When the sun went down, a huge
Calvin Klein ETERNITY logo
appeared on the horizon.
It was perfect."

"If you come back from your vacation
with your cell phone not even broken,
that means it wasn't that great."

"We don't discuss politics, religion,
or Gucci's latest men's collection."

"What's the protocol when you see someone
arriving with a new nose?
Do you congratulate? Say nothing?"
"You say nothing."

"Where's the Chanel emoji?"

"She's not very photogenic
but that's normal.
You can't photograph drama well."

"She goes to McDonald's to buy sliced apples.
Can you imagine the monster
you have to be to do that?"

"She acts clingy as if
she didn't have an ego.
Yesterday her dentures were biting my ankle.
She wouldn't let go."

"He's got a heartbreaking business."

"I don't know if she can read but she's a poem."

"The inspiration is a boy without friends,
in his room."

"The gel you gave me at the gay pride is a wonder.
I put my back out that very night."

"She's hilarious.
The problem is that she doesn't know it."

"Oh look, a drone!"
"No, it's a bird."

"Do you prefer sex or social media?"

"Oh no, you really shouldn't go in August.
It's super lewd, it's full of French people."

"She is not very discreet.
She learned to whisper in a helicopter."

"Yes, I'm looking at Grindr, but don't worry,
I'm listening."

"A petit-four, sir?"
"What is it?"
"Caviar hot dogs."

"That's a brilliant manicure.
During the grunge era,
she was the best at doing dirt
under the models' nails."

"She's such a mythomaniac that being aware of
her existence makes YOU a mythomaniac."

"She's an art collectrisse."

"You don't look your age."
"I haven't taken drugs for years. That's why."

"The music of the fashion show was what
the devil's dentist listens to."

"Be careful. The floor is slippery
because of the champagne."

"Aren't you hot in your tweed dress?"
"It's not a dress, it's a diet."

"I left the party
when the tonic was out."

"Miuccia Prada is the counterintuitive queen."

"Do you have some natural ketchup?"

"Why keep it simple
when you can do better?"

"Kate Moss is looking for you.
She's in the smoking room."

"He's got plenty of ideas but none are his own."

"Yesterday, I was stuck in the Eurostar train
with no air conditioning.
I thought they were trying to make fries out of us."

"Oh, you know me,
the more absurd it is, the better."

"She has a one-thousand-square-foot terrace
that overlooks the Eiffel Tower, but frankly,
her neighborhood is lousy."

"Oh no, don't wear white shoes with a white T-shirt.
You don't want to look like a Q-tip."

"She puts makeup on like a horn."

"Proust? The most I read by him is every month
on the last page of *Vanity Fair*."

"The party was so good that no one
had time to take a picture."

"I'm going on vacation in ten days!
Only two collections to finish!"

"His biography can be told in four emojis."

"The fuses of his modesty tripped
a long time ago."

"It's a piece of clothing that was designed
with software, with no dimensions.
You look as flat
as the screen we designed it on."

"Can you teach me how to cry in Italian?"

"Where are you going this summer?"
"Lebanon."
"Clinic or holiday?"

"If it already exists, I'm not interested."

"It must be hard to reach the peak
of your career at twenty-five—and to be twenty-six."

"That's the eternal problem:
Why wear ugly clothes?"

"What is the inspiration?"
"Wikipedia."

"My new assistant is coming from the thirty-fifth century."

"It's difficult to meet someone
that's on my creative level."

"We need a Periscope celebrity
for our media plan."

"You didn't answer my email
about our new, rare calfskin bag."

"I managed the casting all day.
I wanted to throw burgers
in their faces."

"But why don't you do anything?"
"Because the technology to do
what I want to do doesn't exist yet."

"You have to incorporate the word *love*
into your vocabulary.
I know, you're Parisian,
that's tough."

"How was the fashion show?"
"Banal with a twist."

"I wanted to present a new perspective
on the male suit,
so we put the jacket resting over the shoulders."

"I was at his funeral.
There were only Italian princesses and masseurs."

"I'm fifty-five and looking for a guy my age—
except the rockers are all dead,
only the golfers are left."

"I love her. But I'm warning you,
she only talks about dermatology."

"I'm using my Apple Watch
as a timer for cookies.
It's great."

"Mentally, she's a selfie stick."
"Physically, too."

"She doesn't look like her mother at all."
"Of course, different plastic surgeons."

"My boss just gave me two hundred dollars
to go 'buy me a beer.'"

"He is infinitely useless and infinitely annoying.
He's dust in the company's eye."

"It was last year."
(describing any event from more than two weeks ago)

"She gets bored quickly.
I organize eight- to twelve-minute meetings for her.
The ideal would be four minutes with people
who disappear like on Snapchat."

"Did you like the fashion show?"
"I hated each and every part of it
but loved the whole thing."

"He organized a nice party for the opening
of his new store in Saint-Tropez."
"Who was there?"
"Just him."

"You are sexy this morning.
You look like a young Bernie Sanders."

"The person who created shade is a genius."

"You have to draw us fifteen skirt proposals for tomorrow."
"What's the brief?"
"I don't have the permission to tell you."

"How many hours did it take
to make her wedding dress?"
"Half an hour."

"Twenty-three is the new thirty-three.
And vice versa."

"Don't say *stupid*, say *genius*."

"You are a black hole of energy.
You take everything
and you give nothing back."

"Where does she live?"
"In front of a mirror."

"Did you put your makeup on while having
a phone call with your other hand?"

"He's multilingual: He can say Vodka Red Bull
in every language."

"I couldn't sleep with him.
He is radiant.
He lights up the room.
But I'm beautiful in the dark."

"Love is having dinner without a cell phone on the table."

"No, you don't understand.
It's a noncommercial ad."

"Her hair is too black
and her mouth is too red.
She looks like a charcoal grill."

"How old are you?"
"My spirit is now."

"He talks all the time.
All the time.
I've never seen someone so spammy."

"In the office, they only eat sushi.
We call them the *sushettes*."

"I love your dress.
Don't give it back."

"My theory is that he wears
dog clothes."

"I had dinner with her.
She only talked about filters and likes;
she's completely Insta-centric."

"She's cold and empty
like an Italian luxury boutique."

"She says *yum yum* before she takes
an Ambien."

"I'm looking for jeans that make you look
both sad and sexy."

"Dress for the guy you want,
not the one you have."

"I don't read books, they might influence me."

"People are ugly."
"If they were beautiful,
they wouldn't need our clothes."

"I bought this country house
for the breathtaking sea view.
I'm a Pisces so I love the water."

"No, I didn't see the Valentino show.
There were too many photographers outside.
I was posing for two hours, and I missed it."

"You're from the 15th arrondissement of Paris?"
"Yes, how did you know?"
"The accent."

"Your glamour is my spontaneity."

"Don't say *vulgar*,
say *disruptive elegance*."

"What do you want to do when you grow up?"
"Nothing."

"His hands are occupied by his phone,
so he educates his children with his feet."

"I slept with him during the London fashion shows,
and the next morning he asked me
for an invitation to Burberry."
"Thirsty . . ."

"Gisele Bündchen approached Zaha Hadid to chat,
but there were 220 Korean girls wearing Chanel
screaming around them.
That was the selfiecalypse."

"My life is so exciting and hectic
that I love seeing you on the weekends.
It makes me feel a bit normal."

"I wanted to be an architect,
but it takes too long to build a house,
so I make clothes. It's quicker."

"I was sexually bored.
He was a single shade of gray."

"She doesn't know simple joy.
She only likes complicated joys."

"I haven't read your book
but the cover is very pretty."

"Fashion without fatigue is not fashion."

"He's not a has-been, he's a never-was."

"She came to the office today with bare skin."

"I wanted to build a house with Tadao Ando,
but each time I was refused the permit.
I bought three lots with no luck."

"I really want to make
a poison garden—
only poisonous plants."

"Donatella is talking to me on WhatsApp.
Her profile picture is her portrait
by Helmut Newton."

"When she was a little girl,
she had Tiepolo's frescoes in her room.
She didn't like them,
so she would put posters over them."

"The story is good
so I don't care if it's true."

"I have a passion for hammocks.
There should be a word for that."

"He was an artist but, poor him,
he turned into a money machine.
It's awful when that happens to you."

"The makeup inspiration for the fashion show
was girl who forgot her door code."

"It was a great party—
you felt you were in Paris, but not this year."

"We sell fifteen thousand copies of our magazine,
but only to EIPs."
"EIP?"
"Extremely Important People."

"She was famous for fifteen seconds."
"Like everyone else."

"Hello, I would like some tea,
but not too hot."

"I am unable to concentrate
on anything but my phone.
Text me if you want me to listen to you."

"If it's not complicated, I don't give a fuck."

"What does she do for a living?"
"She pretends."

"Give me thirty seconds.
I have to write this week's editorial."

"It's so ugly.
It looks like a piece of clothing from next year."

"My job is to create the stimulus, you know."

"Our offices are in front of a Celine store.
You can't imagine what torture it is."

"Don't say *mean,*
say *vice president of global communications and marketing.*"

"We lived in a world with just us two.
We thought we were important."

"What's important when growing up
is to keep your pessimism intact."

"I'm an interior consultant."

"You remind me of myself
when I was beautiful."

"What's a French sentence I should know?"
"*Tu as parfaitement raison.*
If you say that,
they will love you."

"She is totally awesome,
but you must not meet her."

"I don't walk, I shop."

"You should buy.
Money is cheap right now."

"I wish I was a slut.
Life would be easier."
"Even more of a slut than you are, you mean?"

"Stop complaining.
You know, Cara goes to New York three times a week."

"Reassure me.
I'm being ass-paranoid."

"She gave the intern grief about choosing which
of her vacation houses she would go to on the weekend."

"Where are we having dinner?"
"This one restaurant in Lincoln Square."
"Oh no, Lincoln Square is far from everything!"

"She's his press agent.
She still tells the story of the one time he was nice to her.
The tale is fifteen years old."

"Wait, I'm watching the sunset
on Skype with a friend who's in Sri Lanka.
I'll call you back."

"I don't buy clothes. I'm sent clothes."

"I don't know how to sew.
For my first collection, I used double-sided tape
for the hemming, and after that, I created jobs."

"The outside world is so violent. I need beige."

"Where did Kanye West come from? Chicago?"
"From the Balmain show."

"There should be a law against yellow shoes."

"The fashion show was amazing.
His interns are incredibly talented."

"It was a photo-sleep party.
You come in, you take the picture, and you go back to sleep."

"She exudes fashion, not health."

"I just broke a twelve-thousand-dollar vase."
"That brings good luck."

"I can't stand her.
I can't help it.
It's a Darwinian reflex."

"What's the trend?"
"Stupid."

"His life is getting into the elevator,
pressing one, and looking at himself
in the mirror while he waits."

"Naomi pushed Cara,
who tried to tear off Naomi's wig,
but it was too well-taped and nothing budged."

"Don't say *repetitive*,
say *true to the DNA of the house*."

"I had dinner with Kim Kardashian.
Let's say we have very few things in common."

"Don't say *boring*, say *sublime*."

"There are so many fashion people
in the restaurant that we're eating
in the *Vogue* table of contents."

"This is the power of fashion's legendarities.
Is that a word, *legendarity*?"

"What do I do with all the bouquets?"
"Take a picture of them with the cardboard box,
and I'll do the thanking afterwards."

"I'm not a snob, I'm Parisian.
There is a very small difference."

"Monsieur Arnault arrives at 1:15 PM,
and the fashion show starts at 1:20 PM."

"She charges for her smiles."

"I'm exhausted.
I'm just a hologram of myself."

"What parties are you going to tonight?"
"All of them!"
"Ah, I forgot that you're not invited
to Celine tomorrow morning."

"It was not bad but it was not good."

"I have so many ideas that I can't sleep."

"I used to change six times a day,
and the media said it was too much."

"Oh, I ate at lunchtime. Too bad."

"You tell me when I have to quit this job."

"Who was at that fashion show?"
"It was fifty percent bloggers."
"And the rest?"
"Female bloggers."

"I hope I die before the apocalypse.
I don't want to see everything in ashes and all.
Too heavy, you know what I mean."

"Paris is a party.
Paris is a hangover."

"They slim her arms so much in photos that
I don't recognize her in real life."

"He has zero taste and zero taboos.
He will go far."

"Celebrity is unbearable.
I don't have a daily life anymore."

"The sky is *pas la* limit."

"She is our muse."
"Ours, too."
"Was she nice on the photo shoot?"
"No. She doesn't have much time to be nice anymore."

"It was good; it was not poetic.
I'm sick of poetry."

"These are dresses that whisper.
There are too many dresses that scream."

"Don't say an *ordinary dress*,
say a *functionalist wardrobe*."

"What is this gray?"
"The rigor."

"The idea was a woman
who had just been struck by lightning."

"You look very beautiful today."
"Thank you, but all the credit goes to the machines."

"I wear black but I drink white."

"It's funny how she doesn't realize that
her big, shapeless snakeskin handbag
is a metaphor for herself."

"Her house is an H&M museum."

"Can you imagine being Kim Kardashian's shrink?"
"We're all kind of Kim Kardashian's shrink."

"I don't have my phone with me.
I left it to charge with my driver,
who's driving around the neighborhood."

"I was second row at H&M but front row at Dior."
"The god of fashion is playing with your ego."

"I hate white."

"Pass me the champagne
to wash down the foie gras, please."

"There are three welcoming places in your lives:
home, work, and our goal
is for the third to be our shops."

"What's a world where you can't say
what you think about the color of the skirts?
When it comes to freedom of speech when dealing with futilities,
we've hit rock bottom."

"He's like Tom Ford in 1999."

"It's natural mink."

"What school did you go to?"
"Tumblr."

"Her walls are white with black baseboards
so it looks like the packaging of Chanel No. 5."

"She's carefree."
"She's V-E day."

"I'm a little bit on edge."
"Let's have a drink and compare our edges."

"Don't I look fat next to the Christmas tree?"

"I'm better. I came to realize
that I was the one I was waiting for."

"She adores me.
I think she confuses me with someone important."

"It's a tribute to Colette and her writing."
(talking about tea)

"It reminds me of the time I cleaned
the bathroom myself."

"Hush, I'm listening to the tree."

"Happy Chanel!"

SEASON 2016

"We're in permanent fuse-blowing mode."

"Don't say you've lost something,
say it's been preempted by time."

"Look! A model who eats.
Film it!"

"I dress in the most boring way possible
so that I don't get photographed
by the hordes outside of the fashion shows."

"He's a collector—of portraits of himself."

"These people don't live,
they Instagram."

"Rome and Hermès didn't happen in a day."

"He asked his assistants to sleep
in the clothes from the collection
to give them a worn-out look."

"I just broke my foot on a Ruinart crate
that was lying around my house."

"They come from all over the world to Paris,
and they turn their backs on the Eiffel Tower
to take selfies."

"See how Mercedes never moves aside?
Well, she's a Mercedes."

"She's super simple.
She goes to the restaurant in jeans and a T-shirt,
no bag, no jewelry, just a bodyguard."

"Ah, it's you!
Sorry, I didn't recognize you
without a Chanel suit."

"Geographically, to her,
Bulgaria is on Place Vendôme."

"Her face looks like an orange Chesterfield sofa."

"She confuses her dresses with reality."

"I gave the duty to one of my interns,
but I don't remember which one."

"What's the opposite of deep?"
"Not deep."

"She is forty years old but she's beautiful."

"Don't say she had bad taste,
say she doesn't know the rules, that she's adorable."

"Did she give herself a facelift?"

"He sucks, but his trick is to
postpone the meeting ten times.
In the end, you feel like you are meeting the messiah."

"The entire front row looked like
Jennifer Lawrence. A surgeon
must have sold the mold."

"I'm flabbergasterned."

"The new insult is 'it was fresh.'"

"This is the third collection
that I've presented since the beginning of the year,
and I have three more to finish
by the first week of March."

"She is not hysterical.
She is concerned about her image."

"What's your job?"
"I warm up the jewelry
before customers try it on."

"Where did her fortune come from?
"She gets royalties from vulgarity."

"What is that jacket?"
"It's Balmain but light."

"What's your mailing address?"
"I travel a lot, so the easiest way
is to ship to Gagosian in New York."

"He has a thousand press agents
but he's stayed super accessible."

"My glass is empty.
Can you pass me yours?"

"They are a legendary couple—
like Yves Saint Laurent and Michel Berger."

"You're beautiful!"
"Oh, you know, it's just skin and bones."

"Sorry, can you repeat that?
I didn't quite get it with the sound of your bracelets."

"You just put your hand on an ass
you'll never have."

"She's a smidgen of very vulgar."

"I swear it's true. Kim Kardashian told
Olivier Rousteing who told me."

"She has Snapchat beauty.
You must not look at her for too long."

"You know, I don't live in the real world,
so who cares about my analysis . . ."

"I don't have keys.
House staff, you know.
And that's a good thing
because I would lose them."

"Do you want a detox juice?"
"No, I'm going for a beer.
I don't want to disturb my body."

"She's an important VIP."

"That's an oxygen gray."

"What makes her laugh?"
"Models crying."

"Yes, he's completely crazy,
but the day you have to design six hundred dresses a year,
you'll be crazy too!"

"Did you hurt your hand?"
"Yes, by opening the invitations for the coutures shows."

"How do we say *wardrobe* in French?
The *garderobe*?"

"How about doing it all in diamonds?"
"That's smart."

"Do you have a cold?"
"No, I swallowed a feather."

"Merci so much!"

"Don't say *déjà vu,*
say *completely trendy.*"

"It's a book that's a quick read,
perfect for a Paris-Milan trip."

"He is extravagant.
For him, when the dress reaches
the end of the catwalk,
the train has not yet left backstage."

"For him, the upside of being this stupid
is that he doesn't know it."

"Am I bothering you?"
"No, it's fine. I was thinking about Prada."

"Greek gods are the inspiration."
"For the white shoe?"
"Yes."

"I hate him like clouds on a Sunday."

"Paris is my catwalk."

"She reads on paper."

"She works a lot."
"You're confusing work and neurosis."

"Who is the photographer? Brice Weber?"

"My shoes have magical powers."
"Not really. We can still see you."

"She's nice, but she has a bit of a
mass-market body."

"These pants look good on you.
Where did you find them?"
"Thank you. I don't remember if they're H&M or Dior."

"It's a week with seven Mondays."

"Being good isn't enough anymore.
It has to put everything else out of fashion."

"It was so great that I don't remember a thing."

"Your socks are beautiful."
"They are warm and light."
"Like you."

"Versace is my North Face.
I feel warm in it."

"Your fear of failure keeps you from having success."

"She takes Ubers to go buy bread."

"I'm as bored as the white orchids
in high-end jewelry stores."

"My boyfriend did a thesis about Molly."

"I'm not perfect but I'd rather have happiness than beauty."

"Everything is changing."

"Nothing to say?"
"I'm having an uncontrollable fit of laughter inside."

"You have incredible energy!"
"I'm like everyone else, you know,
staging and suffering."

"I'm in Miu Miu from last year.
Don't look at me."

"She lives at Castle Monologue."

"He makes the wrong choices, at the wrong time,
for the wrong reasons.
That's why he's always ahead
and completely brilliant."

"He's beautiful like a Ferrari in the sun."

"I'm not a literary person.
I'm not a scientist.
I'm fashion."

"You are beautiful."
"No more than usual."

"It's too hard to write by hand. There is no spell checker."

"He adores you."
"Yes, I left him no choice."

"How's work?"
"You know, perfection is hard."

"I have an incredible need to not give a damn."

"I got a call from a French number.
I almost didn't answer but thought it could be *Vogue Paris.*"

"I taped the unretouched photos Steven Meisel took of me
to the fridge and put a padlock on the door."

"How can I do something new today?
Do you know how irritating it is?
You can't imagine."

"See how Hermès never has a sale?
Well, it's the same with her and empathy."

"It's a lipstick called Apocalips."

"I love lightlyness."

"He travels as much as you get bored."

"I saw you were having a good time last night."
"That much?"
"Let's say you're never going to be president."

"What do you prefer?
Kissing them or making them cry?"

"When she wants to know the time,
she sends a courier to look at the clock
on the village steeple."

"I work in TV, which means I do what you do in your spare time,
but on a salaried basis."

"We work without a garbage can in the studio;
none of them are pretty enough.
We're not going to work with an ugly trash can,
that would be the beginning of the end."

"We don't say *gold watch*,
that implies too much.
We prefer to say *sun watch*."

"I started today. The boss said to me,
'Hello, are you the new one?
Hope you don't pass out like the other one.'"

"I fell on the catwalk once,
and Donatella said to me,
'Who falls? Just the stars, not normal people.'"

"This is a minimum wage × 1,000 coat."

"I was on vacation in the Amazon.
The lightning was really bad."

"One syllable: no."

"Don't cry. Think about your makeup."

"I did the ass casting for the commercial.
You can't find small, muscular, cardio asses anymore.
They all have Kardashian asses now."

"Do you have an iPhone in your pocket
or are you happy to see me?"

"How was your lunch?"
"We had the contest for who had the crappiest week.
Everyone won."

"My wife left me.
She told me I was on my phone too much."

"Who's his muse? La Fée Caca?"

"What day is it?"
"How am I supposed to know that?"

"I think his name is Johnjo—
something complicated and simple at the same time."

"What are you wearing?
Something copied by H&M?"

"So tell me about this dinner."
"I only said things I had already said
and listened to conversations
I had already heard."

"For the form, we need an ID photo of you,
but a selfie will be perfect."

"I want real."

"So, the fashion shows?"
"It felt good to see crazy people."

"I ate a box of macarons after Chanel."

"I have so many clothes at home that
I can't open the door anymore."

"Pharrell was flirting with me again this morning at Chanel.
What a drag."

"I have the same dress as you,
but it's in a different color, a different material,
and a different length—
but it's exactly the same."

"I don't draw. It hinders my research process."

"Remember the old lady
who died during a fashion show in New York?
They didn't stop the show.
If you fall, we go on."

"She lives on the Champ de Mars.
Poor thing has the Eiffel Tower in her living room;
it's way too bright."

"She asks for ten thousand dollars in cash
and ten thousand dollars' worth of clothes
for a photo on her Instagram.
And of course, everyone plays along."

"Your bag is a Saint Laurent?"
"Yes, obviously. Why are you even asking?
Are you stupid or what?"

"Hello!"
"Hello! I'm Anna!"

"It was good to have dinner with you.
Nice to see you not on drugs."

"She doesn't have any more ideas.
Her brain makes the sound
of a straw sucking the bottom of a Coke bottle."

"I have great gossip but the source is unreliable.
Do you want to hear it anyway?"

"I liked it. It was weird
but it was the good kind of ugly."

"I miss Helmut Lang."
"He doesn't miss us."

"I'm sick."
"Have some champagne."

"It's too competitive, and it's silly to believe
that you can still impress with clothes—
so now I do fashion performances."

"I've just come back from Madrid.
I was very disappointed
with the Velázquez Palace."

"A black silhouette is a blank page."

"Kris Jenner is in the second row at Dior."

"I love you."
"Not enough."

"It's embroidered in 360 degrees:
You can't sit down,
you can't bend down,
you can't say no."

"For the fashion show, we spent a fortune
on sublime benches but no one saw them."
"That's the problem when you sit on it."

"They flew me first class to Milan
to put me in the second row."

"I don't like anything."
"You really need a fuck."

"Kanye wrote me a ten-page email."

"I lost my phone at Jacquemus,
but you can contact me via Facebook."

"No interview. He's sweating."

"He's never read a book,
not even the ones about him."

"The inspiration is Audrey Hepburn in khaki."

"Our CEO is spreading rumors
so the designer
who renegotiates his contract will understand
that he can be replaced in a minute."

"I don't dress the women you see in tabloids,
I dress those you see in biographies."

"Anna had a green python trench coat at Jacquemus."

"What's good about their shops?
The real estate location."

"Are we sure about black lipstick?"
"One hundred billion percent sure.
It's super today."

"So how is your man doing—
the one you met in Berlin two weeks ago?"
"We parted ways.
Everyday life killed us."

"He thinks he's smarter than Google."

"He's being very aggressive this morning.
Approach him with the camera on so he'll be nice."

"Can you send us the three questions
you are going to ask him?"

"Do you have a dozen Tylenol, please?"

"She has two pleasures in life:
dressing a lot and undressing slowly."

"I have to do the Gucci review.
Do I look for a new approach
or just copy and paste from my previous write-up?"

"The last thing she thinks about
before going to bed is herself;
it's the first thing when she wakes up, too.
And in the meantime, she dreamed of herself."

"She thinks Birkin is just a bag."

"He's our age."
"Do we agree that we're twenty-seven?"

"I don't take the elevator because it's convenient,
but because there's a mirror."

"I don't recognize him. Who was he originally?"

"Don't say *ridiculous*, say *unique*.
Don't say *ugly*, say *surprising*.
Don't say *old*, say *classic*.
Don't say *stupid*, say *young*."

"Countess Greffulhe was too afraid
to seduce men with her incredible
eyes, so she stared into the haze."

"This hoodie is selling so well
that if we really met the demand
we could make one million a day—
but this is a limited series."

"We make too many collections that when we sell out
we won't have any more ideas."
"What do you do then?"
"Like everyone else, we copy Miu Miu."

"Walk as if you were
angry to walk."

"That's almost one hundred percent true."

"Have you booked a room for the weekend in Berlin?"
"No need. We don't sleep."

"When I arrived, this fashion house was asleep,
forgotten by God."

"Their idea of utopia is themselves: rich."

"They met at the Royal Academy of Antwerp.
They were in-house models for each other."

"I've just come back from Tel Aviv. It was cool;
it was good to see less soldiers than in Paris."

"I'm nervous and depressed."
"Welcome to Paris."

"True luxury is not caring
if your phone is at two percent."

"He's a Red Bull philosopher."

"Those are pants that are ugly with shoes,
but barefoot, they're sublime."

"With me, every day is the day of Saint Butter."

"My rainbows are bridges
while yours are barriers."

"David Hockney painted my portrait today.
I'm gorgeous."

"I think if young me met me today,
she would spit on me."

"I'm not fat. I have American bones."

"She's like you and me,
but I've never heard her talk
about anything real."
"Really like us, then."

"The best thing is to go back and forth
between Paris and Los Angeles in the same day.
There's no jet lag, your body doesn't have time to understand."

"So how's your new fashion job?"
"It's like an infernal vacation."

"It's not a job, it's a life."

"Does she live in Paris or New York?"
"Seat 1A."

"I love her left eye
but her right eye is heavy."

"She wears the New Gucci but with Old Gucci style."

"I don't understand him when he talks.
It's through loose bits of sentences and words . . .
He talks like a mood board."

"What's your trick against blank-page anxiety?"
"Change projects."

"He's totally amazing but you can't
talk to him. He's not a spokesperson."

"She has everything but time."

"It takes six weeks to make our magazine,
which is a monthly issue.
I'll let you calculate the problem."

"In France, we have a problem with people."

"She was awful two days ago
and nobody wanted her.
But since she had an exclusive at Prada,
she's become a Rolls-Royce."

"I was at the Givenchy party.
There were only guys out of this world."

"I think I was born at eleven
because I don't remember anything before that."

"I hesitate between these two dresses."
"This one looks like the curtain at the Palais Garnier
and the other at the Opéra Bastille."

"She never says it's sublime.
She waits until three people with a death wish say
it's sublime, and then she says it's sublime."

"What did you think of the New York fashion shows?"
"New York no longer exists."

"This is my new criteria to
know whether a party was good or not:
If there are abandoned Chanel bags on the floor, it's great."

"How was the party?"
"There were abandoned Chanel bags."

"Say, you look like you're in great shape."
"Yes, I ended up eating."

"He's talented but he has no motivation."

"A skirt is never too short."

"My mom was a shopping freak.
I think I was conceived in a
Paco Rabanne dressing room."

"I love your look.
I'm jealous of your simplicity."

"Don't say *messy*,
say *surprising pell-mell*."

"It's a watch designed like a
silk ribbon that tells the time."

"Your fashion show is in a few days?"
"Yes, we're eating yogurt without a spoon."

"She didn't want children.
Hermès doesn't make diapers."

"I didn't go to fashion school but I have an instinct."

"Your place is lovely.
It's a nice change from the white box I live in."

"They called the editorial staff to force us
to go to their party.
They're advertisers so we were handcuffed to the cocktail bar."

"He's an aesthete.
If he had books,
he would arrange them by color."

"He explained to me that his castle was
cheaper to maintain than a yacht."

"He does not say that a woman is rich,
but that she's beautiful."

"I prefer the *idea* of Beyoncé to Beyoncé herself."

"She works out so much her body should pay her a salary."

"He is the mattress of all of Paris."

"But where does she come from?"
"I don't know, but in any case her clothes come from China."

"One idea is not enough. You need three
and then combine them together."
"No, it's the other way around.
We just need an idea and will use it for one hundred years."

"Go ahead. Stop thinking.
If you fall, you break a tooth. You don't care,
you fix it."

"They think boredom is chic.
They're very chic."

"He doesn't even pay the celebs.
He sends them boxes of dresses—that's all—
and they come to the show.
Friendship is as easy as three free dresses."

"She's fashion dead."

"Everyone copies Richard Avedon so much
that I always feel like he's not dead."

"He's a dandy.
He's wearing his socks without shoes."

"My favorite music is hearing you breathe."

"*Elle* loved it."

"If we think about the future,
we won't do anything.
So we just go for it without thinking."

"Don't say announcer, say *brilliant*.
Don't say *meh*, say *we love it*.
Don't say *confused*, say *full of ideas*."

"Don't say *conservative,*
say *a dive into the archives of the house.*"

"Don't say *unwearable,* say *avant-garde.*
Don't say *indecent,* say *game of transparencies.*"

"Don't say *annoying,* say *headstrong.*
Don't say *he's unbearable*
with his collaborators, say *resolute.*"

"I can't put on this dress.
It's prettier than me."

"For the show, if the back wall is white,
that's intellectual fashion.
If it's black, it's spontaneous and rock 'n' roll,
and the girls will be walking fast."

"I know they're all inspired by their mothers,
but she was inspired by her mother's curtains, right?"

"Don't say it's for gun dealers' wives,
say that the brand is opening a lot of new stores."

"Don't say she was fired,
just praise the successor."

"I did everything spontaneously.
I never would have imagined that
it would become legendary."

"I am excessive in everything,
but I don't have an ego. I promise."

"I don't have an Instagram account.
Well, there is one in my name,
but it's my brand's account."

"Unfortunately, her narcissism
is not proportional to her talent."

"Chanel is not an adjective.
If you write that a tailor is very Chanel,
we are getting sued, and that's not Chanel at all."

"You have to reach that incredible stage
where nobody can criticize you anymore.
Rei Kawakubo of Comme des Garçons is there."

"Catwalk clothes are ridiculous in stores and vice versa."

"Remember, they only buy our clothes to have sex.
Vulgarity is not an issue."

"I threw my suitcase over my head and
wore what fell onto my shoulders."

"I walked out of the show.
It lasted more than twenty minutes.
I couldn't take it anymore."

"Don't you have an idea for a new blue?"

"He gives us sketches of dresses that are
always worn by starving creatures,
with just a pencil line to make a leg."

"Really, my flaw is sincerity."

"It's better to have broken dreams
than no dream at all."
"With that mentality, you should work
at the White House."

"He never touches a piece of clothing nowadays.
He thinks his job is giving interviews."

"The collection is so dark that
he has to work in a dungeon."
"Or a backroom."

"All the people who took drugs
in the seventies are dead;
only boring people
and those who took notes are left."

"How do you say trillion in French?
Don't look at me in a sneering way!"

"She makes herself assistant tartare at noon.
It gives her energy and preserves the figure."

"I like to absorb the chaos and spit out
something beautiful and solid
that sends us toward a future."

"He never takes the easy way out.
That's why we hired him."

"I've just been told our turnover
on belts and had a nervous fit of laughter."

"We make art for rich women."

"It stays afloat thanks to the straw
he sticks in the skulls of fashion school interns and
sucks up every morning."

"She's a little iconic but she doesn't matter."

"Who is that?"
"She's got a fourth-row head."

"Did you sleep?"
"Yes, for two hours.
And I dreamed that I was not sleeping."

"You only think about yourself."
"So what?"

"That's vulgar but an OK type of vulgarity."

"He's amazing.
He's a pastry chef with abs."

"She's beautiful. We could make her ugly,
but she would still be beautiful."
"It's kind of what we do, isn't it?"

"I've decided that after this weekend
I will quit drugs."

"Your scarf! Don't tie the knot
in the middle of your neck, it's too literal!"

"He won't give an interview.
He will only take pictures with celebs
and selfies with clients."

"There's nothing like a fashion dinner
to make you feel super normal
and good about yourself."

"He turned twenty-eight two years ago in Berlin
and now he's forty."

"It's a Levi's T-shirt,
but we credited it to Prada because we don't have
enough Prada credits in the issue.
The readers will manage."

"It's so beautiful that it puts everything else out of fashion.
I want to throw myself in the trash."

"I don't want to criticize but it's a little bit hideous."

"She has a very crinolinian mentality—
none of her ideas go through the doors."

"Your sweater is scratchy."
"Yes, but it's Saint Laurent."

"What was your inspiration this season?"
"We did a pink collection
because people love pink clothes."

"She's Spanish.
Her 5 PM is your 9 PM."

"Walk like your mother just disinherited you an hour ago
and it didn't matter."

"How was your modeling party?"
"Annoying. There were too many exes."

"You don't care what they think.
Walk in like you're a Parisian woman."

"What medicine is he taking?"
"I'm not sure, but his pharmacist must be rich."

"She has everything,
she wants even more."

"He thinks he's a Buddhist because he drinks
green tea and has a receding hairline."

"It's a city shoe—
with a frayed edged and dissonant lacing."

"It was torture, like hearing
the same Selena Gomez song twice in a day."

"It's not exactly black.
There is a subtlety in the darkness, a little pink."

"She's mean, but it's because
the hierarchy is mean to her.
You have to understand her, poor thing."

"He keeps pushing neutrality."

"He was brilliant.
You have no idea how brilliant he was,
but he fell in love and became invisible."

"These reproaches against fashion!
As if fashion should be blamed for everything.
The candy industry is blamed less!"

"It's full-time nothingness."

"I prefer Instagram to Twitter.
I've always been more fashion than word."

"In management, he's like a fork
in a turned-on microwave."

"She looks like Kate Moss but ugly."

"I have friends who can't afford
the $2,000 dress by Proenza Schouler,
but they can't resist so they buy it."

"It's scented with rose but a modern rose."

"These clothes make no sense.
No one will ever wear them.
And we're all so hysterically
out of touch that we don't even say it."

"What's the job of the lady
with the bunny ears and yellow coat—
the one that everyone photographed
in front of the fashion show?"

"Her fleshy sheath is sublime
but she has no grace.
She'll take great photos but no chance for the catwalk."

"Anna smiled at me at Chanel."

"Park right in front of the entrance.
My feet are too sore to walk six feet."

"Do you wear haute couture?"

"Yes."

"What does it change?"

"Everything."

"He hates both injustices and people."

"She's time rich and cash rich."

"Wait, I'm at the airport and my phone needs
to go through the X-ray.
I'll slip it into the thing
and get back to you right away."

"I don't make dresses above $100,000.
My clients wouldn't understand."

"So how was your hookup?"
"The morning one was a pain,
but the midday one was amazing."

"He's ironclad boring.
It's a horrible form of boredom."

"We don't talk about noses anymore.
All the focus is on the cheekbone."

"I was pressured so I made dresses,
but really, I'm an architect without a building.
Well, I designed my stores."

"He's a skin sculptor."

"This baby is so beautiful.
He should be modeling!
Have you thought about it?
No, seriously!"

"Looks like a giant bonsai."
"Yes, it's a tree."

"He gets Amandaleporized."

"He says horrible things all the time.
I got ear cancer because of him.
Seriously."

"He's gorgeous, but I looked at his old profile pictures
and he was ugly before.
Do not date him, he will be ugly again."

"On his head is written:
Strong Potential for Sexual Intercourse."

"My mind is blank.
I'm fashioned out."

"You should open a nicely decorated
psych clinic in front of my workplace."

"And on this rack is our pre-collection,
which is not made by our designer but is a hit."

"Having children ruined his focus.
It's such a shame."

"I have a new boyfriend. He's sexy,
but he needs media training to learn
how to stop repeating himself."

"I just put on jeans this morning.
A little bit of truth feels good."

"Don't say *pretentious* and *unwearable*,
say *it's a demanding piece*."

"This dress took three hundred hours of work."
"Your workers are slow."

"She lives in a cloud of her own creation."

"I had a shitty day
but now I'm feeling really good."
"How come?"
"I changed outfits."

"How is your return to reality?"
"What reality are you talking about?"

"I want to buy a pack of cigarettes."
"But you don't smoke."
"I want to start."

"I taught philosophy to my nephew."
"What concept did you start with?"
"Champagne bubbles.
They don't just come from the bottom of the glass."

"We wanted raw refinement,
so we put nails on the cashmere."

"I would like them in size 42."
"We have them in size 42 at our Montaigne store.
I'll bring them to you by taxi.
Have some champagne while you wait."

"I've been working for him for three years.
Three hundred sleepless nights.
This morning he told me again nice to meet you."

"She said we had to water her dresses—
and that meant making us cry."

"I don't like being called a fashion designer
because I hate fashion.
I'm a dressmaker."

"I'm not ashamed of anything.
It would be a waste of time and I'm in a hurry."

"I didn't want rules
because they define endings,
and I only like beginnings."

"Nobody cares about
a designer who eats noodles at home,
so he has public whims
that make him look like a creative."

"For social networks, we want content that stops the thumb."

"I went on vacation to Brazil,
but everything inspired me too much
so it wasn't real vacation."

"I wore the dress inside out by mistake,
but the result was a lot more interesting."

"He's a journalist but not a very good one.
He's not perverse enough; I even think he's nice."

"I hate ballet flats—
except if it's Chanel."

"She's a miracle."
"*Cour des miracles* or Miracle by Lancôme?"

"I'm doing nothing.
I even procrastinate my procrastination."

"Instead of actual walls, he installed paper walls
so that employees whisper,
creating a church vibe around him."

"She's as interesting as an invitation
for a show that already happened."

"She sent me three terabytes
of emails that were declarations of love."

"The inspiration is a rich woman who has become poor
but still spends lavishly."

"It really is effortless sophistication, you know."

"Hello, I'm stuck in traffic.
Can you wait for me and delay the beginning of the show?"

"Your coat is awful.
Did you forget that you were part of the visible world?"

"The key is not to think about what I have already done
but what I will do again."

"Don't say she's fired,
say she's leaving the company
to devote herself to a personal publishing project."

"I am sensory handicapped. I can only wear couture."

"How was your weekend?"
"I'm exhausted from love."

"There are limits. They're not human,
but there are limits."

"I check Twitter, Facebook, Snapchat, and Instagram,
and when I've seen everything, I start over.
I keep doing that until the day is over."

"He gobbles up assistants by the dozen.
He's the fashion military service."

"We prototyped a sublime new bag,
but now it has to open.
The studio is looking for a solution."

"Oh my God!"
"But God who?"